PREVIOUS BOOKS

Spiritual Wisdom for Peace on Earth From Sananda
Channeled through David J Adams

LOVE is the **KEY.** Part 1
Spiritual Wisdom from Germain
Channeled through David J Adams

LOVE is the **KEY.** Part 2
Spiritual Wisdom from Germain
Channeled through David J Adams

WE ARE ALL ONE
Spiritual Wisdom from The Masters of Shambhala
Channeled through David J Adams

ENLIGHTENMENT AND ILLUMINATION
Spiritual Wisdom from Djwahl Khul
Channeled through David J Adams

COSMIC SYMPHONY OF LOVE
Spiritual Wisdom from Hilarion
Channeled through David J Adams

THE NEW EARTH

SPIRITUAL WISDOM FROM

THE MERLIN, AR'AK, and SPIRIT OF CRYSTALS AND GEMSTONES

CHANNELED THROUGH

DAVID J ADAMS

authorHOUSE®

AuthorHouse™
1663 Liberty Drive
Bloomington, IN 47403
www.authorhouse.com
Phone: 1 (800) 839-8640

Published by AuthorHouse 10/04/2019

ISBN: 978-1-7283-3042-6 (sc)
ISBN: 978-1-7283-3040-2 (hc)
ISBN: 978-1-7283-3041-9 (e)

Library of Congress Control Number: 2019915755

Print information available on the last page.

The Front Cover Sacred Geometry is called the "The New Song for the Earth". It has been painted and photographed by Kaye Ogilvie, Intuitive artist from Queensland, Australia, and based on a description channeled through David J Adams.

Back cover Photo was taken on the camera of David J Adams, the T shirt was created by Tie Dye artist, Ruth Cary Cooper from USA.

This book is printed on acid-free paper.

DEDICATION

I Dedicate this book to my children, Nicky and Suzi, my grandchildren, Lauren, Matthew and Emily, and my great grandchildren, Ruby–Rae and Peyton, for they and others of the next generations will carry the Light forward and create the Peace that we all yearn for.

ABOUT THE AUTHOR

ADAMS, David John Patrick

Born: 28th April 1943

At: Mountain Ash, Glamorgan, South Wales, UK.

Moved to South Australia in 1971, Currently living in the southern suburbs of the city of Adelaide.

Began his Spiritual Journey as a result of the Harmonic Convergence in late 1987.

In 1991, he was asked by Beloved Master Germain to undertake a global Meditation based on, and working with, the Consciousness of the Oceans, which was called the Marine Meditation.

In 2009 he was asked to address a Peace Conference in Istanbul to speak of the Marine Meditation and his work for World Peace through meditation.

He is a Songwriter, a Musician, an Author and Channel, but most of all a **SERVANT OF PEACE**.

David began bringing through information from a variety of Masters and Cosmic Beings in the form of Meditations around 1991. It was not, however, until after the year 2000 that he began to channel messages in group situations and in individual sessions. Most of these messages were not recorded or transcribed so remain shared with only a few people, but in 2009 the messages being brought through in the weekly Pendragon Meditation group began to be recorded and transcribed by Kath Smith and sent out around the world on David's own Pendragon network.

David's special Guide and Mentor has been 'The Germain, the I am that I am', but he has also worked extensively with – and channeled - Sananda, Hilarion, Djwahl Khul, AA Michael, The Merlin, The Masters of Shambhala, as well as Arcturian Sound Master Tarak and his own Home Trinity Cosmic Brother Ar'Ak.

(Contact email – djpadams8@tpg.com.au)

ACKNOWLEDGEMENTS

I, David J Adams, would like to acknowledge three special Earth Angels.

Heather Niland/Shekina Shar - who helped me to awaken to my Journey in 1987 and connected me to my Beloved Friend "The Germain", she was a mentor, guide and teacher way ahead of her time.

Meredith Pope – who walked in the same shoes as me in those difficult early years as a fellow 'weekender' at The EarthMother Centre, and was-and still is-an inspiration to me.

Krista Sonnen – An Harmonic and Earthwalker, who helped to build the bridges to my Spiritual and Cosmic friends by persistently urging me to allow them to speak through me in private sessions, then in group sessions. Without her support these messages would not be here.

I would further like to acknowledge **Kath Smith** – A spiritual Being of immense Love and Joy who initiated the recording and transcribing of the messages received in Pendragon so that the messages from our 'other Dimensional friends' would not be lost forever. Also **Takara Shelor,** who combined her Global Water Dolphin Meditation with the Marine Meditation in 1998 and has organized the Marine Meditation website as an adjunct to her own Dolphin Empowerment website ever since. Also **Kaye Ogilvie**, Intuitive Spiritual Artist, who Painted all the Labyrinths walked during the Marine Meditations, as well as many other inspirational images that have assisted my Journey of Growth.

I also acknowledge all those here in Australia and those throughout the World who have supported me and encouraged me over the years, and in particular, **Barbara Wolf and Margaret Anderson**, who's vision and hard work has made this book possible.

BLESSINGS OF LOVE, JOY AND PEACE TO EACH AND EVERY ONE OF YOU.

DAVID J ADAMS

FOREWORD

We Humans live in the concept of "Linear Time', which divides 'Time' into minutes, hours, days, months, etc. and goes in a straight line from 'Past' through 'Present' to 'Future', consequently we give importance to the date on which something happens. Our Spiritual and Cosmic Friends are not bound by such constraints, they operate in the **'Now'** moment, so although the messages within this book have 'dates' attached to them, they are, essentially, **TIMELESS.**

Some messages do, of course, refer to specific events, such as the Equinox or the Solstice, or even some man made event, however, the underlying message is always **TIMELESS.** So we ask, when you read these messages, that you accept them as having importance within the **'Now Moment'** of your lives. Although we have given the date of receipt at the end of each message, they are not in sequential 'linear time' order.

All messages were received within the Pendragon Meditation Circle and always began with the 'Sounding" of the Tibetan Bowls, the Blessings Chimes, the Drum, and occasionally other percussion instruments. Many of the messages make reference to these Sound frequencies.

Let the messages speak to your Heart, for that is what they were intended to do when they were given by **The Merlin, Ar'Ak and Spirit of Crystals and Gemstones**.

Blessings of Love, Peace and Joy

David J Adams

INTRODUCTION

Some of you may be aware of, or have seen, the British TV series called 'Doctor Who', where the central character is a 'Time Lord' simply known as 'The Doctor'. This character periodically takes on a different Human form as he travels to different places in different time zones. Well, *The Merlin* is cut from the same cloth, in that he too is a 'Cosmic Time Lord' that adopts different forms at different times.

Most will identify him with the 'mythological' figure in the Arthurian tales of Camelot and Arthur and the round table, This was just one of his Earthly Manifestations, but the one for which he is most remembered. It may be a 'coincidence' of course that *The Merlin* began channeling through me after my Circle became known as the Pendragon Meditation Circle, because Pendragon was the family name of Arthur of Camelot, but then there really are no coincidences are there, smile.

His messages are about Peace and Love and the 'magic' of the Earth and all who are on the Earth, not surprising as he was always regarded as a 'Magician'. I hope he will enable you to find the Magician within yourself.

Sharing the spotlight, so to speak, in this book is my own Cosmic Home Trinity Brother *Ar'Ak*. It is my understanding that the 'Trinity' is the basic building block of the Universe, indeed many religions of today have at their Heart some form of Trinity – Father, son and Holy Spirit in the case of the Christian Religion,

Ar'Ak began moving messages through me as far back as 1986 – before I recognized my Spiritual awakening – when, without my Conscious awareness, he would slip a few words of Wisdom into letters I was writing to a friend in America. It was later revealed to me that each of us who have come from other Planetary sources to assist the Earth in its Ascension at this time, do so as part of a Trinity. *Ar'Ak* is the 'link man' in my Home Trinity of '*Yrdd*' (The Sound Vibration of my Home Planet),

Ar'Ak is not so much a name but a Sound Vibration, my own Trinity Sound Vibration is *Ra'Zu* (the Z is pronounced as a ts), and the third member of the Trinity who is back on the Home Planet has the Sound Vibration of *Ga'Rut*.

Ar'Ak began channeling through me virtually as soon as I had 'agreed' to channel, although much of his wisdom predates the days of recording and transcribing the messages, so are now 'lost' - as if anything is really lost, smile.

I hope the messages that have been recorded and transcribed and form a part of this book will resonate with your Heart and uplift your Soul, and help you to awaken to greater depths of yourself - after all, it really is all about YOU!

The third member of this "Trinity of Lighted Beings" is **Spirit of Crystals and Gemstones**, who first came to me back in 1993 when I was in my infancy of awakening Consciousness. At that time he or she gifted me 19 meditations on different individual crystals, which we still use within Pendragon today. I say he or she because initially I made the assumption of maleness because the Being was coming through me, but much, much later Beloved Kaye Ogilvie a talented Queensland Spiritual artist was given a vision to paint of **Spirit of Crystals and Gemstones** which turned out to be a beautiful feminine Being. Of course our Enlightened Spiritual friends are all in a ONENESS form that defies male or female stereotypes, so imagine **Spirit of Crystals and Gemstones** as feels right within your Heart, smile. I hope the Wisdom of this amazing Being of Light will resonate with your Heart and Sing to your Soul. Blessings of Love, Peace and Joy.

David J Adams

(djpadams8@tpg.com.au)

CONTENTS

The Merlin

1

.——.

GIVE PEACE A CHANCE

(The circle opens with the Sounds of the Tibetan Bowls and the Blessings Chimes)

Greetings, Dear Hearts, I am the Merlin

'PEACE' is not a 'protest' movement.

'PEACE' is an *'affirmation'* movement

'PEACE' is a way of Being

For too long we – and that means all of us – have allowed Peace to be marginalized, to be perceived and portrayed as some 'way out' concept dreamed up in a hallucinatory stupor by some random band of what were termed 'hippies' in the 1960's. Well, Dear

Hearts, it is time that we woke up to the realization that *'Peace'* is, in fact, our Natural state of Being

'Peace' does not oppose, it creates.

It creates a 'variety' of ways of living, it creates a 'variety' of ways of thinking, it creates a 'variety' of ways of Being.

'Peace' embraces variety, and does not perceive that as 'differences'.

It is only when you perceive 'differences' and create judgements of those 'differences' that you sow the seeds of conflict and war. 'Differences' are a part of the old Paradigm of separation, Variety is part of the new paradigm of Oneness.

Dear Hearts, it is time to let go of the outmoded concept that *'Peace'* merely opposes war – it does not! – Peace replaces war as an acceptable way of Being.

Think on that!!! PEACE REPLACES WAR AS AN ACCEPTABLE WAY OF BEING.

Wow, how crazy is that!!! or is it???? IF you accept that *'Peace'* is not a poor relative of other ideologies, but has simply become so because we have allowed it to be so, then *We can change it!* not tomorrow, not next week, not next year, not next century, but *Right Now!!!*

How??? by *'affirming internally'*, and *'expressing externally'* that

> *'Peace is my natural state of BEING'*

and then

Living that belief in your daily lives

As we move into Global Oneness Day on 24th October, let us all embrace the 'variety' in our lives that *'being Peace'* provides, and reach out to all our brothers and sisters on the Earth Planet and say:

Welcome Home …….. Give Peace a Chance

Blessings of Love and Peace.

(23rd October 2013)

2
. —— .

IT IS NOT THE DESTINATION THAT IS MAGICAL, IT IS THE JOURNEY ITSELF

(The gathering opens with the Sounds of the Tibetan Bowls, the Blessings Chimes and the Drum)

Greetings, Dear Hearts, I am the Merlin

When people hear my name they think immediately of wizardry and Magic, and indeed on my many incarnations on the Earth Planet I have been involved in many magical happenings, but this is not because I have special energies or talents, I have, in each incarnation, the same energies and talents as all other Humans, but when I incarnate I am One with the Earth, I am One with what you call 'nature', and I open my Heart and my mind to embrace the magical energies that I know are part of everything upon the Earth Planet.

You too can be part of magical happenings upon the Earth if you set aside your limitations and become One with the Earth and with nature, for it is within the Earth and nature that magic happens. I sense that some of you are shaking your heads and looking around and saying *"What magic? I see nothing"*, Dear Hearts, you need to look with your Hearts, and you need to open your Hearts, and you need to accept the 'Knowing' within yourself, that *everything upon your Planet is Magical,* for what you see, Dear Hearts, is all to do with your perceptions, you only see what you perceive, and much of Humanity perceives only the outcomes, the end product, you might say,

So I ask you, Dear Hearts, to think just a moment, about going out into your garden and perhaps planting a bulb, and tending that bulb, and in the fullness of time from within that bulb emerges a beautiful flower, *How magical is that?* Think also of the dragonfly who is birthed in water but comes to the surface, changes its appearance and flies, *How magical is that?* But when you look upon the flower or you look upon the dragonfly you do not think of how they have reached that state, and the magic involved in that. You see, this is part of the Earth, this is part of nature, you know it is happening-somewhere in the deeper recesses of your mind-but you do not perceive it as magical.

Look at Humanity, Dear Hearts, look how babies are conceived, and grow within the mother, and are birthed, *This is Magical.* Dear Hearts. Just because you are not seeing every step of the journey does not rob the journey of its magical energies. This is why you need to open your Hearts and open your minds to the 'knowing' that everything is magical.

You have recently talked of some of this, Beloved Germain came and spoke to you about 'silliness', and he used the baby as an example, when you watch the baby exploring its new environment. Last week at this very Circle you spoke of your childhoods, the 'magical mystery Tours', the 'Road trips', and you wondered why, suddenly, you had been shown these parts of your past, Dear Hearts, *it was to enable you to see more clearly that it is not the destination that is magical, it is the journey itself.* Every step of the way magic happens around you and within you.

As Spiritual Beings you know about the *'journey'*, but even so, you speak of ascension as if that was a destination, when in reality it is simply a part of the *'journey'*, but if you focus your intention upon ascension as the destination, you ignore the magic of the journey that leads you to that point, or the journey beyond that point. *Magic is perception.*

The whole of nature is magical, a seed is dropped into the earth and from that seed a great Oak tree will grow, *is that not magical?* So, Dear Hearts, look around you, find the magic in everything you see and everything you do, and you will find that your life will take on a new meaning, a new glitter, you will find that you are not depressed as much by the shadows that are projected to you by your TV screens.

When you are asked, as you often are, to go out into nature, it is for a reason, and the reason is to open yourself to the magic of what is happening all the time upon the Earth Planet. *This is an amazing, amazing Planet,* with so much to offer you in the way of learning and growth, so why do you consistently diminish that opportunity by looking only at your destination, and ignoring the journey itself?

If you Perceive, you will see the magic all around you, and that magic will lift you higher and higher into your Soul Dimension, for when you see the magic behind what is happening in your world at this time, nothing is limited any more,

So whether it is a dragonfly that you see flitting past, whether it is a butterfly - do not simply focus on the butterfly but remember how the butterfly came to be, a caterpillar became a chrysalis, a chrysalis became a butterfly, *These are Magical Energies at work!!!*

It is time, Dear Hearts, for each and every one of you to start working with these magical energies, You cannot work with these energies if you do not recognize them. If you deny yourselves the ability to see and to accept that magical energies exist everywhere, in every tree, in every flower, in every animal, and, Dear Hearts, in every Human Being.

Look for the magical energies in all around you, and open your Hearts and your minds, and you will work the same magic that people assume The Merlin makes, and it has been said to you before in channeled messages,

"EMBRACE THE MERLIN WITHIN YOURSELF"

For I am One with the Earth, with nature, and I am One with You.

Dear Hearts, embrace the MAGIC of Yourselves.

(30th September 2016)

3

.——.

'SHAPE SHIFTERS'

(The Circle opens with the Sounds of the Tibetan Bowls and the Blessings Chimes)

Allow the Sound vibrations to shake loose the last vestiges of shadow within your Being, enabling you to become the true Light Being that you are, for the shadows are of yesterday and the Light is of the NOW, and it is time for all Beings upon the Earth Planet to accept and acknowledge the Light within themselves, the Light within their Hearts.

Imagine yourself as a ball of brilliant Light, and imagine Mother Earth taking your Light into her Heart and embracing you fully and completely. Feel uplifted by her embrace, feel empowered by the beat of her Heart.

Greetings, Dear Hearts, I am The Merlin.

As Humanity, through the ages, has become more and more creatures of cities, of concrete jungles, they have lost their deep connection with Mother Earth. It is a bit like animals in the wild becoming animals in a zoo, when you live in your glorious cities you perceive nature in such a way, captured in small areas, and you look at those small areas but you do not relate to those small areas. You can, however, embrace Mother Earth within your Heart, *for unless you become more connected to nature, to the Earth and to the Oceans you will lose your Souls.*

Think about that, Dear Hearts, life upon the Earth is a Soul journey, a journey of the Heart. Gradually through eons of time you have severed your connection to nature. As the Earth moves forward in her Ascension it is important to begin once more to embrace your connection with the natural elements of the Earth, with the trees and the forests, with the Oceans. These are not small areas of recreation, these are the Heart and Soul of the Earth.

In the earliest of times you were all *'Shape Shifters'*, you were Human and you were animal, you were trees, you were flowers, you experienced each as a part of your life, you became the eagle soaring high into the sky and seeing the panorama of your Earth, you became a worm burrowing beneath the surface, discovering, uncovering, the essence of the Earth. You became the dolphins and the whales journeying beneath the Oceans, and you became Humans walking upon the Earth, but in those earlier times you were *totally* connected to the Earth, this is what enabled you to be *'Shape shifters'*, for you still possessed the knowledge, the magic if you like, of your energetic Being as opposed to your physical Being.

The changes that are taking place upon your Planet at this time are calling your Hearts back to the time of the *'Shape Shifters'*. The energies that will flow into your Earth Planet at the time of the Equinox will provide the key to your Heart, to open yourself more fully to your Energetic Being, which in turn will allow you once more to change your form and become the other aspects of the Earth.

When you are told, Dear Hearts, *'You are all One'*, this means just that, you are all One - *the tree, the plant, the dolphin, the whale, they are all a part of you and you can be in their form at any time.*

Many people are frightened at the thought of someone changing shape, changing form, and yet there is nothing to fear, for you are merely expressing that you are **all One.**

You have confined yourselves to your cities, physically and mentally, and although you will continue to physically reside in your cities, you are being given the opportunity mentally to explore the reality of all being 'One' upon the Earth.

Oneness is an amazing state, one within which you can be everything you wish to be. You are all aware of the changes that are taking place upon the Earth at this time, for some they are troubling, for some they are magical. *It is up to each of you to choose which perspective of the changes you hold in your Heart - you choose between fear and Love.*

If you choose fear you will draw back into yourself and become isolated from the Earth, but *if you choose Love you will be expanded* and you will embrace the wonderful opportunities of being *One* once more with Earth Mother.

We have asked you tonight to perceive yourself as a ball of Light being embraced by Earth Mother, becoming a part of Earth Mother, enabling Earth Mother herself to become **EN-LIGHTENED**, and *we ask you to commit yourself to this permanently*, to utilise the energies coming in to the Earth Planet at the time of the Equinox to open your Heart fully and share the Love and the Light that has always lain within,

WAITING TO BE AWAKENED!

(17th March 2015)

4
.—.

EMBRACE THE MERLIN WITHIN

(The Circle opens with the Sounds of the Tibetan bowls, the drum and the Blessings Chimes.)

Open your Hearts to the vibrations of Love and Light that fill this Circle this evening, penetrating every aspect of your Being, uplifting and enlightening, filling each part of you with the wondrous energy of joy and ecstasy. Feel the beat of your Heart in rhythm with the beat of the Heart of the Earth, unifying, completing the cycle and circle of your life as you move inexorably into the Higher Dimensional Frequencies of Divine Love, Divine Peace and Divine Joy.

Greetings, Dear Hearts, I am The Merlin.

I come tonight to remind you that you are each Magical Beings capable of transforming yourselves in many, many different ways. You tend, Dear Hearts, to perceive yourselves in a single physical vessel, you look in your mirrors and you see yourself and you judge yourself and yet you are seeing but one aspect of yourself. You are capable of transforming yourself into many, many different Beings of Light. You fly with the Angels, you walk with the animals, you embrace the trees, and you become each and every one of those things.

You perceive your life as being a duality of 'awake' and 'asleep', but this is not so, you are eternally changing, transforming, transmuting, becoming different *'Beings of Light'* in each and every moment of your day, for while your physical vessel moves about and performs its tasks within your physical realm, there are so many other aspects of yourself that are in other parts of your Earth, doing different work, encouraging, enlightening other Beings, contributing to the global Ascension process.

I wish to encourage you, Dear Hearts, to embrace the Merlin within each one of you, for yes you are *ALL* Merlins, you are all magical, you are all transformatory Beings. Let go of this perception that you are but a single vessel, a single vehicle, acknowledge and accept your Multidimensionality, both within, upon and beyond the Earth Planet.

Once you embrace the Merlin within, you become the Oneness of all things, you begin to communicate with the trees, with the plants, with the animals, with the Oceans, for they too are also a part of you. *You are not limited by your physical incarnation.* No, it simply gives you roots upon the Earth, but from those roots grow the Cosmic Tree.

So take a moment and imagine yourself expanding, embracing every aspect of yourself. Let go of the limitation of your physical body, embrace your energetic Being and allow yourself to fly with the Angels, to walk with the animals, to swim with the whales and dolphins, to be a part of All that is upon the Earth and beyond the Earth.

Do not limit yourselves to the duality of 'awake' and 'asleep', know that always you are many things; you encompass the whole of the Earth and the whole of the Universe. *You are Light beams that seem to have no substance, and yet they are capable of creating,* and you cannot create where there is no substance.

BE the Merlin, acknowledge the magic within yourself, practice the magic within yourself. Do not seek to direct it with the limitations of your mind, **let it soar,** gift yourself in all your many manifestations to the Universe, to the Earth, to all that need your Light. **BE** the magical Merlin of ancient times, and **BE** the magical Merlin of **NOW.** **Let yourself soar into the Light Being that you truly are, the magical rainbow of life, each colour a different Dimensional Frequency in which you exist, in which you work, in which you play.**

It is time, Dear Hearts, to break down the barriers of limitation, the barriers of duality. Move within your Heart to every part of the Earth, communicating - with your Light and Love vibrations - with all the other Beings that inhabit the Earth, that surround the Earth, for you are all a part of the *ONE,* you are all

'THE MERLIN'

(24th November 2014)

5

. —— .

TAPESTRY OF LIMITATIONS

(The circle opens with the Sounds of the Tibetan Bowls and the Blessings Chimes and the Drum)

Greetings, Dear Hearts, I am the Merlin

The central theme of recent messages has been to be true to yourselves, and not accept limitations on yourself from others or even from your own self. *Limitations are learned, they are not part of your reality.* Your reality is total freedom and total abundance of Spirit. So it is time to focus upon yourselves, to honour and give thanks for who you are, to let go of all judgments that you perceive are coming from other people, to see yourselves through the eyes of your Soul instead of the eyes of others, because as we accept the powerful Cosmic energies that are flowing into the Earth at this time, we need to be able to flow with those energies in a balanced and harmonious way. We cannot do that if we continue to accept limitations of self. We can always find other people, other things, other lives to blame for the limitations we have within ourselves, but as always the reality is that it is something we choose, and we can choose differently.

So I invite you now to move into your Heart and consciously dismantle all aspects of limitations within yourself, from this lifetime and your many lifetimes on this Planet, *and the limitations you brought with you to this Planet.* It is time to let go of everything that limits your perception of yourselves as anything less than perfect, anything less than perfect *'Source'* energy.

Imagine for a moment that you are sitting within your Heart chakra, and in front of you there is this tapestry that contains all of those things in your existences that have created limitations in your life. Instead of sitting there and admiring the beauty and the complexity of the patterns of limitations that have been created, reach out and begin to unravel that tapestry. Undo the first knot, and then gradually draw the threads from that tapestry, the threads you have laid down through your many lifetimes, the threads you have accepted as part of yourself, when in reality they have been imposed upon you by circumstances, by events and by emotional responses. *It is time to create a new tapestry of Light, a tapestry that is vibrant and alive with potential, with possibilities, a tapestry of Light.*

But first take the time to unravel the tapestry of your limitations. There will be moments when you will look at the tapestry in front of you and you will think "I don't wish to unravel that particular part, it looks so beautiful", and yet you know that these are your *Limitations*, however beautiful they may appear, they are your limitations and it is time to unravel them and let them go. So look at the patterns in front of you, all of them, and then dismantle them, piece by piece, thread by thread.

As the tapestry begins to shrink, your Consciousness begins to take control and begins to weave and weave and weave a new tapestry of Light, a tapestry without limitations, a tapestry that is perfect in Balance and Harmony. A tapestry containing all the elements that you need for your journey ahead – Love, Joy, Peace, but most of all, freedom from limitation.

So now as you unravel one tapestry, you are simultaneously creating another, and you find yourself looking less and less at the tapestry that you are unravelling, and looking more and more at the beauty of the tapestry you are creating. It becomes easier and easier to unravel the old, to let go of your emotional connections to the limitations which gave you a sense of safety, for the realization grows that ***the safety comes from your freedom, not your limitations.*** Continue to unravel the tapestry of limitations and create the tapestry of Light, and feel the shift of energies within your Heart ***from one of burdens to one of lightness.*** Feel your whole Being begin to rejoice and pulsate with a feeling of blessedness, a feeling of empowerment, a feeling of enlightenment, and your energy begins to move faster and faster as you weave and weave and weave this new tapestry of Light. You are re-weaving yourself, creating a new vibrational frequency within yourself that can absorb more and more Light.

As you weave your new tapestry of Light, Sound into it the joyfulness, the Love, the Balance and the Harmony. ***Sound away the old, and Sound in the new.***

As you reach the last thread of your tapestry of limitations, undo that final knot that holds you to your past. *Give your blessings and your thanks for all that has been to this point in time.* Move your focus totally to your new tapestry of Light, *give it your blessings and your thanks for all that is yet to come,* for you have accepted your true Divinity, you have opened yourself to all that is. This tapestry will absorb more and more Light, and enable you to reach into more Dimensions of yourself. Give it the life of your Consciousness and your intent.

Now look at yourselves again and see who you really are! Free of all limitations! Free of the shadows of fear! Complete in the golden Light of Divine love.

You are the weavers of your own reality!!!

And so it is.

(29th March 2010)

6
·——·

MAGIC IS A WONDROUS
ENERGY CREATED BY LOVE

(The circle opens with the Sound of the Tibetan
Bowls, the drum and the harmonica)

Greetings, Dear Hearts, I am The Merlin.

The Equinox has opened many gateways to other
Dimensional Frequencies, and you are being invited
in each and every moment of your day to journey
into other Dimensional aspects of yourselves.

For once again, Dear Hearts. I remind you that
Dimensions are not outside of yourself, the
Dimensions are within and the gateways also are
within, for everything leads to the deepest parts of
your Heart and to the deepest aspects of your Soul,

for you are the creators of today, and the creators of tomorrow. ***You are the Magicians.***

Yes, Dear Hearts, you may look around your world at this time and see the darkness, feel the pain, and you may wonder how these things happen when you are being directed so frequently to ***Be*** the Love that is creating the New Earth. But what you see, Dear Hearts, is all the illusions of the past, reminders if you like, of what you used to be, but they are no longer enfolding you in their *'hands of fear'*.

Have you noticed, Dear Hearts, how you are now looking out at these things and not becoming embraced by the fear of them, but simply observing them and continuing to radiate forth the Love from within your Hearts?

This, Dear Ones, is how the higher Dimensions function. They take away the emotion of the events that you are facing, and therefore they take away the fear. You observe and you Love despite what you see. In the past, Dear Hearts, you have only been able to Love if what you were seeing was Loving, but now you find you are quite capable of radiating forth Love from your Hearts, even when beyond your physical Being life seems to be chaos.

Eventually, Dear Hearts, you will not need to look out beyond yourselves and see these illusions of darkness and chaos in order to be able to perceive the changes within yourself. *You are in transition, moving between Dimensions.* At times you will be in your old duality world, but you will react to it differently because you have lifted your Hearts and your Souls into higher frequencies of Light, and you know deep within you that by being Love, you are gradually changing the vista outside of yourselves.

You may feel at times that progress is slow, but Ascension was never intended to be an 'instant thing'. You are still bound within your linear time, you continue to exist in your linear time, therefore it seems that things are moving more slowly than in reality they are.

> *The truth Dear Hearts is that you have already changed*
>
> *You have already expanded your Hearts*
>
> *You already reside in your Soul Dimension.*

This is the magic of the moment. Some of you may recall walking through those structures that had different types of mirrors and seeing yourself elongated, or extremely fat, extremely short, and it made you laugh because you knew that this was an illusion, but you still enjoyed seeing yourselves in all these different situations. And so it is now, Dear Heart, your old world is a world of mirrors, and as you walk at times through the old world you see yourself in a different Light, in a different shape and now you can look upon yourself in those different guises and you can feel Joyfulness, for you know that what you look at is an illusion, perhaps the way you used to be, perhaps the way you wanted to be.

These are all mirrors of you, and the whole of your world is a mirror for you, and you choose which of the visions you see, you embrace and take into yourself and react to, but more and more, Dear Hearts, you are reacting only to the Love within your Hearts, and you are seeing more and more the effect on the outer world of the radiance of that Love from within your Heart.

It may not be every moment of every day that you see only the Love within yourself, but every day in more and more of those moments you will be seeing the effect of Love on those around you, and those across the whole of your world, for as you move into higher and higher Dimensions you become the *'Masters of your Magic'*.

Magic is a wondrous energy that is created by Love! so do not become frustrated, Dear Hearts, do not beat yourselves up for your perceived lack of progress, Know with absolute certainty that you are not what you were yesterday or the day before, you have changed, you have expanded, and every day you embrace more and more Love and Light, and you become more Love and Light, and the whole of the Earth begins to resonate in Harmony.

Take time each day, Dear Hearts, to move inside yourselves and *tend the garden of the future within your Hearts, and watch that garden grow into a magical world filled with wondrous Light and Love.*

Blessings be upon you, Dear Hearts.

(24th March 2014)

7

.——.

WELCOME HOME TO YOUR ONENESS

(The Circle opens with the Sounds of the Tibetan Bowls and the Blessings Chimes)

Without opening your eyes, I ask you to embrace the Light flickering on the table in front of you, sensing deep within yourself the myriad of colours the Lights project, bathing yourself in Light, feeling that Light deep within your Heart, uplifting every aspect of your Being, feeling the denseness melting away, as the Light of Higher Dimensional frequencies radiate through you, reaching deep inside and finding the magnet of the Light at the centre of your Being.

For you are a magnet for all Light, a storage unit for all Light, a receiver and a transmitter of all Light, and as you embrace and radiate that Light, the denseness, the heaviness of your Being is melted away, and you feel yourself becoming ONE with your Higher Self, embracing your 'Soul knowing', embracing the highest frequencies of Divine Love.

The more Light you attract into yourself, the more Light you radiate forth. The more Light you radiate forth, the more you change your environment. As you change your environment by en-lightening your environment, you begin to create the New Earth of Divine Light and Divine Love.

Greetings, Dear Hearts, I am The Merlin. I am delighted and excited to be sharing with you at this time the monumental change that is taking place upon the Earth Planet.

I refer to you as 'Dear Hearts' because now we speak only to your Heart, for your Heart understands what your mind cannot comprehend. Allow all words, all images, all visions to move through your Hearts.

When we speak to you of change, we do not speak of a single event. We speak of a gradual process of evolvement, a movement into the higher forms of Light and the deepest most radiant forms of Love.

Because it is an evolvement, Dear Hearts, it is not an instant change. There will be times during this, and future years, when you will be moving in and out of new realities and old realities.

Change is subtle but powerful, and we have sought in recent messages, to address some of those changes – changes in perspective and perception, changes in attitude, all of which grow and begin to create the changes that will become perceptible to most upon the Earth Planet.

One of the major changes, Dear Hearts, is the movement from your mind into your Heart as your guidance system for the remainder of your time in your physical vessel, and you will find that many things occur in your lives that do not make sense to you, and your mind will continue to say "why?, or, what does this mean?" and I ask you, Dear Hearts, to bring that down into your Heart.

It is not necessary for your mind to understand. Everything that is brought to you at this time in your lives is part of your journey of Ascension, and once you know this and accept this, you lose the need to understand and give meaning to what is occurring.

Treat them, Dear Hearts, as miracles within your lives. Do not try to judge them on the basis of what has been in the past, for these are all a part of your coming together into Oneness, for that is another aspect of the change – the movement from Duality into Oneness, the movement from Separateness into Unity.

You are bringing together your multi dimensional selves into Oneness. You are beginning to embrace your soul families once again, and although your mind may not understand how this will operate, accept it, allow yourself to flow joyfully with what will be occurring in your lives.

Do not hold onto fear. Do not hold onto pain. Embrace the Light within your Hearts, and see all that occurs within your life as a part of the joyfulness of your existence.

Many of you will know through your mythology that the Merlin is an arbiter of change, a practitioner of magic, but ***the magic is within each and every one of you, Dear Hearts.*** It begins with the Enlightenment within your Heart, and it manifests in changes in your path - changes you may not have foreseen, but changes I invite you to embrace with great Love, with great Joy, *for there is no going back to the old ways. Look always forward through your Heart.*

We have given you this message many times in this linear year. Look at your life through your Hearts. Do that now.

Embrace the Light within your Heart,

Radiate that Light, that you may co-create the path ahead of you.

I can assure you, Dear Hearts, the journey will be worthwhile, for the time of separateness is past, and we of other Dimensions reach out to embrace you, and we say

"WELCOME HOME TO YOUR ONENESS".

(28th May 2012)

8

·———·

THE HEART IS TAKING CONTROL OF THE PLANET

(The Circle opens with the Sounds of the Tibetan bowls and bell.)

Greetings, Dear Hearts, I am the Merlin

Allow your Hearts to open wide - your Human Heart and your Higher Heart, embracing the Sound Vibration of the bowls, and allowing those vibrations of Sound to uplift your Heart into the essence of Joyfulness.

We are approaching a time of a new influx of Cosmic energy at the time of the Solstice, and once more this will be the energy of "understanding".

Understanding is of the Heart, not of the mind- for understanding is that deep inner knowing of what is appropriate, what is right, what resonates deeply for you.

That also applies to the Earth Planet itself, so the inflow of "understanding" energy that will take place at the time of your Solstice will be received by the Earth in two places-*at Glastonbury, the Heart chakra of the Earth Planet – and at Hawaii the High Heart chakra of the Earth Planet,* activating both the physical and the Spiritual Hearts of the Earth.

Through these two places the energies will flow along the Rainbow Serpent Songlines to all the corners of the Earth – the Outer Earth and the Inner Earth.

The Earth itself needs to understand its place within the Cosmos, that it may then unlock the wisdom that it has held since its inception, for the wisdom of the Earth is as critical to the new vibrational frequencies as is the wisdom contained within each and every one of you.

I ask you now to focus your attention on these two important inflow areas, both of which are areas previously considered to be areas of the **Goddess energy** - for the Heart understanding has always been perceived by Humans as a Feminine frequency. *Now it will be a frequency of Oneness* – the coming together of the Divine Feminine and the Divine Masculine into a *'Oneness of Understanding'*.

The energies will awaken the Avalon of past times and the ancient energies of Lemuria - for the Heart is taking control of the Planet itself and all upon it.

As you move towards the Solstice – open your Human Heart and open your High Heart, and connect these to the places mentioned - to Glastonbury and to Hawaii - for each of these exists within you, and you will feel the inflow of the powerful energies of Understanding, and the wisdom that exists within you now will begin to be revealed fully, and you will finally understand all the things that you know.

Take a moment now to connect yourself with these places, to allow your minds to journey you to the Isle of Avalon and the Isle of Hawaii.

In your mind's eye, see the Gateway open, and the energies of Divine Oneness be revealed to your Heart and your High Heart.

Feel yourself meld into these energies,

Embracing the energy of **Understanding**,

Embracing the **Oneness**,

Embracing the Divine Feminine energy and the Divine Masculine energies,

Becoming the Goddess within yourself and the God within yourself.

When you bring together in Oneness the Divine Goddess and the Divine God, you begin to create the Oneness that you will need in the new Earth frequencies, for the time of separation of these two important balancing energies is over.

Feel the Love and the Joy burning within your Hearts, embracing your minds, consuming your physical vessels. Feel yourself become that Oneness, become that Love, become that Joy.

This inflow of energies from the Cosmos will take place over a period of time surrounding the Solstice-so

Allow your hearts to remain open,

Allow your connection to the inflow points of the Earth to remain open, and

You will feel uplifted and enlightened.

I am The Merlin, and I thank you for sharing your time with me this evening.

(19ᵗʰ December 2011)

9

THE AWAKENING OF THE HEART OF HUMANITY

(The circle opens with the Sounds of the Tibetan Bowls and the Crystal Bowl)

Allow the Sounds of the bowls to uplift your spirits, to embrace the deepest parts of your Heart, and invite into yourself the Sound vibrations of Peace and Harmony. Finding Harmony within your selves is critical at this time, for there are many energies flowing to and from the Earth Planet at this time.

There is much shifting of energies, so Harmonising within your Hearts is important to stabilise these energies, and enable them to be focused. The time of chaos is fast fading, and it is time to look forward to Harmony and Peace on the Earth Planet, and that will only come when you find the Harmony and Peace within your own Hearts.

Greetings, Beloved Ones, I am The Merlin.

Shortly, in your time, you will reach that point of change, the time you call the Solstice, the time when the sun moves in a different direction, a change of direction, and this will signify a change of direction within yourselves.

It is important therefore to focus your energies very clearly on what it is you wish to achieve in this lifetime upon the Planet. Many veils are parting, the Beloved Isle of Avalon is once again opening its gates, moving back into a Dimensional Frequency that is attainable for Humanity.

There are many entrances to the Sacred Isle of Avalon and many Beings of Light will move through these entrances and come together once more to create the magic of the Earth.

This is indeed, Dear Hearts, a time of great magic, and as with all magic, there is more than the eye can see, so do not despair, do not complain about a lack of action, instead express your gratitude for where you are on your journey, for where the

Earth is upon its journey, for these are magical times.

Much is being created behind the scenes, and it is through the Light within your own Hearts that all these things are being created. Even as you watch your T.V. screens and you see the apparent chaos in different parts of the world, look deeper, Dear Ones, look for the magic within each of those happenings and you will see that beneath the surface of even the most chaotic situation, you are seeing the upliftment of Hearts, you are seeing people speaking out with courage, with conviction from their Hearts, and you will see how those striving to hold on to power seek to crush the Hearts that are opening. But as you look, you see more and more Hearts opening, more and more of Humanity standing up for themselves, and for the 'collective' of Humanity.

This indeed is a magical change that is taking place upon your Planet. Give thanks for it, Dear Hearts. Do not judge it all on the surface of what you see, look beneath the surface, look into the Hearts of those involved and you will clearly see the change taking place all around the Earth, an upliftment of Community.

Yes, Dear Hearts, there are still barons who seek to control, but their power is waning, and they are in fear and desperation in the way they react to the Awakening of so many Hearts. *They know their time is done.*

So many beautiful energies coming into the Earth at this time, deep into the Hearts of all of Humanity, the Awakening is gathering force.

Many Light Beings are gathering at the Sacred Isle of Avalon for the time of the Solstice, a time when they will unite in their Hearts and focus upon the change of direction on the Earth, *the Awakening of the Heart of Humanity*.

Do not focus on judgment and fear, focus instead on Gratitude and Love, and feel the power of Light within yourselves, and open your Hearts and share that Light with all those around you, for it is the power of the *ONE* that will create everything.

(17th June 2013)

10

·——·

WHAT MATTERS IS THE
MESSAGE ITSELF

(The Circle opens with the Sounds of the Tibetan bowls, tingsha bells and the drum.)

Allow the resonance of the bowls to flow into every aspect of your Being, uplifting and enlightening the essence, the core, of your Being, and move deep within your Heart Chakra to surround yourself with the Light of Love deep within your Heart. Feel your whole Being begin to sparkle with the intensity of this Divine Love within.

Allow that sparkling Light energy to flow out into the world, to Light the way for those who follow behind, those who seek the Light within their own Hearts. Your Light provides them with the impetus to go within, and to find the sparkling Light of

Divine Love within themselves, that they too may share with others.

Greetings, my Beloveds, I am The Merlin, and I embrace you from the Heart of Avalon, and offer you my thanks, my gratitude, for the Divine Love and the Divine Light that you focused upon Avalon at the time of your recent Olympics. I want you to know, Dear Ones, we felt even the smallest amount of Light and Love that was directed to us, not only from within this Circle, but from within the many Circles around the Earth that came together at this time to focus their Love and their intent upon that special moment of Unity, of coming together in Oneness that your Olympics allowed at this time.

There was great Joy and great Love created, and this will now be taken to all the distant parts of the Earth Planet, for all those who came and all those who watched have been infused by the Love of Oneness, the Love of Togetherness, the Love of Unity.

Each one has been awakened in their own unique way, and each one will go from this place a different Being than when they arrived. All the energy of this coming into Oneness flowed into Avalon, and flowed into the many Dimensions of Avalon, and created through this place - and through the grids and Rivers of Energy of the Earth - a new magic. *Joyfulness once again became the dominant emotion of humanity.*

Do not think, Dear Ones, that because your Olympics have concluded that you may now all 'retire'. I am here to tell you Dear Ones that it is just beginning.

We move quickly now into the period that has been spoken of frequently for the last 25 years, the time of Harmonic Convergence. *Think upon those words Dear Ones – Harmonic Convergence - the coming together in Harmony of the whole of the Earth.* Then you will focus once more upon London with your Para Olympics, when once again Humans from all across the Earth come together in Love, come together in Respect and Honour - different athletes, different support crews, all with the same purpose, coming together in Harmony and Unity.

Beyond those Olympics we come to the Equinox and the coming together of Humanity and the Ocean Consciousness in your Marine Meditation. It will be a powerful time, but only if your Hearts are open and focussed on Oneness and Unity.

Beyond your Equinox there will be the upsurge of energetic flow towards the Solstice of the 21ˢᵗ of December – *the time of the Great Shift.*

Powerful times ahead, and during these times you will be encouraged, you will be applauded, you will be assisted, you will be aided. There will be many, many messages from your inter-dimensional friends, and your inter-galactic friends.

We have already spoken to you about perception and perspective, but there is one more aspect of discernment that I wish to address at this time. *Humanity has often made judgement on messages they receive, on the basis purely of who the message is from. It is time to let go of this out dated method of discernment, for it is never the messenger that is important, it is always the message itself.*

It is time, Dear Hearts, to let go of your need for specifics in terms of your messengers, and instead focus on the content of the messages themselves, and allow your discernment to operate purely on the message. It does not matter if the source has a name that you recognise, all that matters is the content of the message and how that resonates within your Heart.

You understand what I am saying, Dear Hearts? *Focus now on the messages you receive, the information that is offered to you, and make your decisions based on the discernment of your Heart.*

Let go the ego need for specific names, specific sources. Focus totally on the messages themselves, for when you do this your Heart will make the decision for you on what is right for you. It will decide on the basis of the Light that is within the message itself.

It is, of course, perfectly natural for you to have your favourites in the sources purporting to put through these messages. How many times, Dear Ones, have you asked or been asked "Are you sure that this is really The Germain, or really the Djwahl Khul"? What I am saying to you now, Dear Ones, is that the question is irrelevant for it does not matter. *What matters is the message itself, and your Heart taking from that message that which it needs.*

We will continue to speak with you, to share with you the wisdom that we may have, and we will also listen to the wisdom that you have, for we have said many times to you *"we do not know more, we simply know different", and when we share our differences we acknowledge our Oneness,* for we are all looking at the same goals - the Ascension of the Earth and all upon it.

There is magic within each of your Hearts.

Use that magic to create the New Earth of Peace, Love, Harmony and Joy.

Blessings be upon you Dear Ones.

(13th August 2012)

11
. —— .

YOU ARE LOVE

(The Circle opens with the Sounds of the Tibetan bowls and the drum)

Allow the resonance of the bowls and the passion of the drum to permeate every aspect of your Being, feel yourself become One with all that is, feel the Light vibrations pulsing through your Heart, through your energy field, through your multidimensional Being, uplifting all into Higher Dimensional Frequencies of Light and of Love. Allow your Hearts to speak to every other Being upon this Planet, creating a "Communion of Love, a Resonance of Joy".

Greetings, Dear Hearts, I am The Merlin.

I come to speak to you tonight, for the time is fast approaching of your festivals, your coming into

Oneness with each other, the time of seeking the Peace and the Joy that this time of your Earthly year creates.

It is a time of moving beyond yourself and embracing others, of opening yourselves in Love to all those around you – to your families, to your friends, even to those you do not necessarily know.

It is a time in your Christian calendar when you seek to rebirth Unconditional Love, and to embrace the *'Unity of Humanity'*, and yes, Dear Hearts, it does not always work out as you intend, but that is a part of your journey. What is important is the intent within your Hearts. *Magic comes from within your Heart. It comes from Self-Love.*

At this time of your year in particular, it is not possible for you to create Love with others if that Love does not exist within your own Hearts, so I come tonight to ask you to take a little time in preparation for your festivities and begin by Loving yourselves completely, totally, unequivocally. Love yourselves, and when you feel the power of this Self-Love filling your Being you will begin to radiate that energy forth, and you will touch everyone else with that Energy of Love.

Of course you cannot command how they react or respond to your gift of Love, but do not let that concern you. Focus totally on the Love within your Heart and simply gift that Love to ALL unconditionally.

It is that last word that creates the main problem with Humanity. You are so accustomed to placing conditions upon your giving, you have expectations of return.

But this, Dear Hearts, is because *you do not Love yourselves enough,* you look upon the return as justification for your giving, because you do not have the self-belief, the self-confidence to simply share the Love within your Heart, because in times past you have not seen, or felt, or accepted that Love within your Heart. You have only perceived it in the reflection that is returned to you.

Do not look to others to be the mirror for yourselves, know with absolute certainty that Love is ALL, and you can gift Love without losing any of that Love, for within your Heart there is an eternal source of Love, once you embrace it.

The magic lies in the word *'Love'*, and it creates miracles upon the Earth. Take a moment and allow yourself to feel, to really feel, the intensity of the Love within your own Heart at this moment.

Do not think about it, do not seek to find an outlet for it, simply feel, really truly feel, the Love within your Heart, and when you do this you become that Love, and a new sense of Bliss emerges. You have left behind the doubts, the uncertainties, the judgments of yourself, and you have simply **become** the *'ENERGY OF LOVE'*.

No one can steal the Love within your Heart, no one can turn it on and off,

You are Love. Accept that truth and your life will change magically.

This is the time to begin your new journey - the journey of self-belief, the journey of self-Love, and far from making you look inwards, Self-Love allows you to radiate outwards with no fear, with no expectations, simply *accepting* that

YOU ARE LOVE

(2nd December 2013)

12

.——.

LIVE REACTIVELY OR
LIVE PROACTIVELY

(The Circle opens with the Sounds of the Tibetan Bowls and the Drum)

Relax, and breathe deeply, drawing into yourself the True Light of Spirit - connecting deep within your Hearts to the powerful Light of your own Spirit. Breathe deeply of the Light.

Greetings Beloveds, I am Ar'Ak - Cosmic Home Trinity Brother of this one, through whom I speak tonight.

I wish to speak to you about the two choices you are faced with at this time of sometimes turbulent changes upon your Planet.

The two choices are - to live reactively or to live proactively.

I wish you to understand clearly what I mean by these terms.

To *live reactively* is to allow the events and happenings outside of yourself to create and colour the energies within yourself – emotional energies, Spiritual energies, and sometimes even physical energies.

To *live proactively* is to create the energies within yourself, and apply those energies to embrace the events and happenings outside yourself.

The differentiation is quite clear.

> In one you accept control of your own energies. *You are proactive.*

> In the other, you give away control of your energies to others. *You are reactive.*

For most of the lives that you have spent in this Dimension of duality, the majority of Humanity has chosen to exist *reactively*. This has made it quite simple for some on your Planet to wield total control over many - whether this is in a physical sense or a Spiritual sense.

As you are moving through these times of transition, those who wield that power seek to continue to dominate your existence. You may speak of these as the dark forces, the darker ones, the evil ones – but this is not so. They are simply Beings who exercise control of their own emotions, and through that, assume dominance over those who do not.

So the light and dark of which you often speak is about the choices you make within yourselves. Think about that for a moment. At this time of great change, many events are happening on your Planet - some you will see, most you will not.

You are all aware that your media is controlled by a small number of people, and that your media feeds you selective information.

There is no judgement made in our Realms on these Beings who create this information.

You have the choice to allow your energy to be influenced, to be coloured, to be created by what is fed to you through your media.

You also have the choice to make judgements of what you see from within the energy you have created for yourself.

Again, in our Realm there is no judgement as to which one you might choose. However, the **_longer you remain 'reactive', the longer it will take to transcend yourself and the Planet into higher Dimensional frequencies._**

It is time now to choose to create within yourselves the Divine Love, the Divine Peace, the Divine Joy of mastering your own destiny.

With these energies firmly in play, embrace all that you see, embrace all that is placed before you with a new awareness, a new knowing. Become **_proactive_** in your life.

The choice will always be yours - to allow others to create your existence (which they do from a **_Love of Power_**), or to create your own existence (which you do from the **_Power of Love_**), and embrace 'all that is' in Divine Love, Divine Peace, and Divine Joy.

As your Planet moves inexorably into higher Dimensional frequencies, you will be called upon to make this choice, day in and day out.

You have come here at this time to make a difference to the Earth.

Can you make this difference by being *reactive* or *proactive?*

That is your question.

That is your choice.

I ask you. Beloveds, to choose wisely.

Blessings be upon you.

Embrace the Divine Light of everyone within this Circle, and radiate that Light out into the world as a beacon of hope for all mankind.

And so it is.

(27th June 2011)

13

·——·

'MISTAKES'

(The Circle opens with the Sounds of the Tibetan bowls and the Crystal bowls)

Greetings Dear Hearts, I am Ar'Ak, Cosmic brother of this one through whom I speak tonight.

I wish to pose a question to each and every one of you –

> How many *'mistakes'* have you made today?
>
> How many *'mistakes'* did you make yesterday, or last week, or last year?
>
> How many *'mistakes'* have you made in your entire lifetime on this planet?

I am sure that if I gave you a pad and a pen you could spend the rest of this evening writing out your list of perceived 'mistakes', and I would look upon them and I would tear them up and burn them, and I would say to you "they are but illusions". For you do not make 'mistakes', you make *'decisions'*, and from decisions flow consequences, or you take *'actions'*, and from those actions flow reactions.

It is only in hindsight, when you perceive what the reaction has been or what the consequences have been, that you make the determination that you have made a 'mistake', so your judgement is based, not upon your decisions or your actions, but upon how they are received by others.

Your decision is never a *'mistake'*, it simply sets in train motion which creates differing responses.

Why am I bringing this to your attention at this time Dear Ones? For a number of reasons, firstly when you create a perception that you have made a *'mistake'*, you open the door to an insidious virus in your energy body, a virus called *'guilt'*, and *'guilt' sucks up the energy within your Being, it calls into question your self-belief, your self-respect, your self-worth.*

If you multiply that virus by each of the times in your lifetime that you have perceived yourself as having made a *'mistake'* and therefore taken upon yourself this *'virus of guilt'*, you can understand how over time you deplete your energy, you deplete your perceptions of self-worth, and as you do that, you draw back into yourself, you lose the desire to make decisions.

In this time of transition, of great change upon your Planet, this is not a time to hold back from making decisions. You need to embrace once more your self-worth, your self-belief, you need to have faith in yourself and the courage to make decisions.

It does not matter if your decision is instinctive or impulsive, or if it is carefully thought out, because you are in a world of free will, you cannot dictate the responses of others, and therefore you cannot necessarily dictate the outcome of the decisions that you make.

So let go of that list of *'mistakes'* that you have in your mind, or in your energy field, or on your pad of paper. Let them go, open the door to release the virus that you have stored within your energy bodies, *"the virus of guilt and blame"*.

Your Spiritual friends have spoken to you often about not judging, and yet you judge yourself all the time, and invariable you judge yourselves negatively. You look at the reactions of others and you blame yourself for those reactions, but you are not responsible for the reactions of others, Dear Hearts, you are only responsible for the reactions of yourself.

That is not to say that you should not be considerate of others, Dear Ones, but having made a decision, you must allow others the freedom to react according to *their* principles, *their* beliefs, to what is within *their* Hearts, to what is *their* journey, but if that is not what you expected, you do not then look back at your decisions and say *"Ah I made a 'mistake'*

No, Dear hearts, I say again, there are no *'mistakes'*, there are only decisions and consequences of decisions, and actions and reactions to those actions.

If you make your decisions based on the Love in your Hearts, *congratulate yourself,* irrespective of how others perceive that decision, *congratulate yourself,* Love yourself, give yourself the confidence to continue making decisions based on the Love in your Heart, and let go of the expectations of other's reactions.

So when I ask you next time "how many *'mistakes'* have you made today?" You say "I have made no *'mistakes'*, I have simply made decisions based on the Love in my Heart, and I honour all who view that decision or receive and accept that decision, I honour their right to react for themselves, for their journey".

Presuming that you have made a *'mistake'* is merely an attempt to control outcomes, when you cannot control outcomes, you can simply be honest and Loving with yourselves.

Are you ready to release your perceptions of *'mistakes'* in your lifetime?

Are you ready to open the door and release the *virus of 'guilt' and blame?*

Are you ready to Love yourselves totally?

(26th August 2013)

14
.———.

LOVE AND LIGHT COMBINE
TO CREATE JOY

(The Circle opens with the Sounds of the Tibetan bowls, drum and the Tingsha bells.)

Feel the vibration of Sound uplifting and enlightening the totality of your Being, resonating not only within your physical vessel, but within all Dimensions of your Being.

Feel yourself as a complete Being of Light in all Dimensions, and allow your Heart to expand through all those Dimensions of Light and Sound and Love.

Feel yourself expanding and becoming a part of **all that is**, letting go of your sense of separateness and embracing Unity and Oneness, and feel the empowered energies of Love flowing through everything, becoming a total Oneness of Love, for that, Dear Hearts, is your true Being – *Divine Love expressed in many forms, in many Dimensions, but all a part of Oneness.*

Greetings Dear Hearts, I am Ar'Ak, Cosmic Home Trinity brother of this one through whom I speak tonight, and I embrace you as part of myself, as part of the Oneness and I invite you to embrace me as part of your Oneness, that we may share the Light together and be One in Love together.

Feel the Light we create together as One, and feel the energy of Love moving through the Earth, moving through the Cosmos – a part of you - a part of me.

Each time we come together in this Circle we empower the Oneness of all. It is part of the journey that each of us is undertaking at this time - a journey of growth.

Growth is an important word for you to consider. For tonight - as was indicated earlier this year-I am bringing forward to you another of your *"pearls of wisdom"* from the past, that you may look upon the words gifted to you previously, with your new understandings and your new awareness.

Many moons ago I came to you and I said:

> *"Knowledge is not growth until you use it to create Joy in your life, and in the lives of others".*

I ask you now to focus on those words, to feed them through your Hearts, and ask your Heart for greater understanding of their meaning, for on the surface they may seem simple, but they carry with them great wisdom on many levels - for in those few words, we have spoken about your purpose in being on the Earth at this time.

It is not to accumulate knowledge, simply for knowledge's sake. If that were the case, Dear Ones, you could have manifested as a dictionary, for that is filled with knowledge, but in itself it has no value until the knowledge within it is released and used by others.

So if knowledge and the accumulation of knowledge is not your purpose on this planet, then it has to be growth, and growth comes when you use the knowledge that you have gained for a purpose, and when you look again at the words we have given you, you will see that the purpose for which you need to use your knowledge is to create Joy in your life, for Joy is the Bliss that comes from understanding and awareness, But again, that is not the sole objective of your life upon this Planet – *you are here to create the Joy for others also, so it is about sharing.*

You are not here on this Planet simply for your own benefit, but for the benefit for the whole of Humanity, and the benefit for the whole of the Earth, for they are all a part of *You.*

I ask you to go back to those words again, and to feed them through your Heart, and to come to an understanding within yourself of the purpose of your existence.

We have spoken much of late about *'discernment'*, for there is much knowledge and wisdom that is passed about upon your Planet, but only some of that will be relevant to your journey, only some of that you can take and use to create Joy in your life.

You can take knowledge and create pain in your life, so again Dear Hearts, *discernment is important.* All the knowledge and the wisdom you come across in books, or you are gifted by others - upon your Planet or from beyond your Planet - all have to be filtered through your Heart - and then used for a purpose!

As we have said before – *energy itself simply exists.* It begins to come alive when it has focus and intent, and that focus and intent comes from within your Heart. So knowledge is an energy, and you select that which is appropriate for your journey. You select that which is appropriate to create a specific reaction within yourself, and that reaction Dear Hearts is Joy-for *Love and Light combine to create Joy,* and without Joy there is no Light, there is no Love, upon your Earth.

So once again focus on those words –

> *"Knowledge is not growth until you use it to create Joy in your life, and in the lives of others".*

I bless each and every one of you and embrace you with my Love and my Joy.

(27th August 2012)

15

·——·

ALWAYS BELIEVE IN YOURSELF

(The circle opens with the Sounds of the Tibetan Bowls and the Cosmic Tone)

Allow the vibrations of Sound to lift your Hearts into Joyfulness. Feel yourself letting go of all the discomforts, negative energies, that you may have accumulated throughout your day, and feel your Heart open, feel the energy of Joy expanding within you, allowing you to see the World around you through a different lens, the lens of Love and the lens of Joy. For everything around you on your Planet is how you perceive it. No two Beings of Light upon the Earth will see the same thing with the same eyes, and the same energy, everything is unique to you. This is why, Dear Hearts, sometimes it is so difficult to explain to others why you feel so Joyful when something happens, when they are seeing the same thing but not feeling that Joyfulness.

Greetings, Dear Hearts, I am Ar'Ak, Cosmic brother of this one, and I enjoy so much joining with you in this Circle, and experiencing the unique energies of each and every one of you. For I have worked with each of you for a considerable length of time, although you may know me by other names, you will always know my energy. But each of you will absorb that energy and see me differently, and that is how it should be, for it is the uniqueness of your own perspective that creates the life you lead.

So being 'different' in the way you perceive the happenings upon your Planet is not a negative thing, it is a positive thing, it is the reason why there are great artists and musicians upon your Planet, because each one sees the world differently and describes the world differently, and there are times when you may embrace what others are seeing and feeling and expressing, and find an affinity with it, and you add to the energy of the other person's unique vision, as they also add to the energy of your unique vision.

You are often faced with the word 'Illusion', and you perceive that to mean that it is not real. That is not what Illusion means! Dear Hearts, an Illusion simply acknowledges and accepts the different perspectives of each individual, which indicates that what is being seen has different meaning and different form to different people. So as no two people see an event or a happening on your Planet the same way, it cannot exist fully, it is an *'Illusion'*. But only because it is seen by so many different eyes, or heard by so many different ears.

Within each one of you there is discernment and there is judgement, so whatever happens upon your Planet is fed through these individual feelings and emotions, and are therefore expressed differently.

What is reality? Dear Ones, reality only exists within YOU. Always accept the wisdom that is within you. You do not need confirmation from others of what YOU perceive. It is quite Human, of course, to seek that confirmation, for you are, in the main, very self doubting.

Everything exists upon your Earth simply through your Vision, through your imagination. This is what makes the Earth Planet such an incredible place to be, such an incredible place to watch. *We are in awe of those of you who have chosen to be on the Earth at this time, for the energy of what you perceive is what is creating the future of your Planet,* and it is a future which is a fusion of all. All the different colours, all the different Sounds coming together to create the Whole.

Each one of you contributing your unique perspective. It is like having a blank canvas and having many people involved in creating a painting on that canvas, each wondrous contribution creating the magnificent whole

So, Dear Hearts, do not allow yourselves to feel negative when someone says "All life is an Illusion", instead, accept that as a compliment to your unique talents, and *__always believe in YOURSELF.__*

I thank you, Dear Hearts, for accepting me into your circle tonight.

(31st March 2014)

16

THE EARTH PLANET IS BECOMING A 'LIGHT STAR'

(The Circle opens with the Sounds of the Tibetan Bowls and the Blessings Chimes)

Imagine that every frequency of Sound is a unique colour and you will immediately become aware that you are surrounded and infused with multiple rainbows of colour, flowing with the Sound deep into the centre of your Being, and you become a *'Rainbow Being'*, and as you do so, feel the Joy that each and every one of those colour vibrations creates within your physical body, within your energy body and within your Multidimensional body. For colour and sound are ONE - uplifting, empowering, creating within you the highest vibrations of Consciousness that it is possible to achieve at this time. For each of you the experience may be a little different, but as a whole the experience is ONENESS - oneness of Colour, oneness of Sound, oneness of Light.

Greetings, Dear Hearts, I am Ar'Ak, Cosmic brother of this one.

It has been a great joy for all of us looking on at the happenings upon and within the Earth, at the gigantic leap forward that the whole of Humanity has taken over recent times. Although many are yet to awaken to the true reality of their Spirituality, many, many Beings of Light upon the Earth have so awakened, and have become receivers of the energies of the Cosmos that have been flowing to Humanity and to the Earth Planet itself.

You are leaving your state of isolation within the Cosmos. You are being embraced more and more each day by other Planetary Systems within the Cosmos. *The Earth Planet is becoming a 'Light Star' in its own right* and there are many now within the Cosmos who will be looking to the Earth for examples on how they too can increase the vibrational frequencies of their Consciousness.

You judge yourselves far too harshly upon the Earth Planet, you see stumbles as failures whereas, in reality, they are experiences that enhance your journey. *You chose to be on the Earth Planet to learn more about form and more about your own Spirituality,* and although it has taken most of you many lifetimes to understand this, the time has come upon the Earth Planet when many, many Beings of Light are coming to this understanding and are reaching out from their Hearts to those beyond the Earth. Just as we, over eons of time, have reached out to embrace you and support you, you are now doing that to others.

You may think, Dear Hearts, that you are in your infancy in exploring the Cosmos because you have this limited perception. In reality, you have been moving frequently around the Cosmos to other Planetary Systems, exchanging information, exchanging wisdom, bringing back to your Earth Planet that which you need and giving to others what they need, but you have done this in a different Dimensional Frequency to your perceptions on Earth.

How many times, Dear Hearts, have you been told that you are Multidimensional Beings? And that is so true, and yet you remain limiting in your thoughts, in your minds. You may acknowledge that you are Multidimensional, but you do not yet accept fully that you are - and always have been-operating within these other Dimensional Frequencies. *You have never been limited to the physicality of the world that your minds are aware of on your Planet.*

You have always moved amongst the Stars, and as you now move into your Hearts and away from the limited concepts of your minds, you are becoming more and more aware of the other aspects of your Multidimensionality, and it is a time of great rejoicing for all those within the Cosmos, and it should be a time of great rejoicing for you upon the Earth Planet. You are moving more and more into the reality of Oneness and the multi-faceted aspects that Oneness is.

You have recently begun to awaken to the reality of the Earth Planet itself being a *'Multidimensional Being of Light'* and that has changed your relationship with the Earth on which you walk. It is no longer simply an object, it is a part of the greater *you* and the more and more that you acknowledge and accept this new awakening into Oneness, the more you will understand about your Spiritual travels and your Cosmic travels.

You have never been isolated and limited solely to your existence upon the Earth Planet. You know that your time in any one lifetime is limited, what you do not know is the time between those lifetimes and whether that has been limited or whether that has been limitless.

It is time to travel deep within yourselves and in so doing you will become more and more aware of your friends in other parts of the Cosmos, you will become more and more aware of everything.

The duality and the separation that you have created as a smoke screen on your Planet is fading rapidly as you begin to embrace Oneness within your Hearts.

Take your time, there is no rush, *there has never been any limitation on what you can do and what you can understand, it has only ever been a question of opening the doors within yourself and letting the Light of Consciousness live deep within your Hearts.*

These are special times for each and every one of you, enjoy every moment of every day and be aware that

YOU ARE ONE WITH ALL THAT IS.

(25th April 2016)

17

·——·

ONE WITH THE HEARTBEAT
OF THE CREATOR

(The Circle opens with the Sounds of the Tibetan bowls, the Drum and the Blessings Chimes)

The Sounds of the Blessings Chimes lift you into a New Dimensional Frequency of Light. Feel yourselves moving upwards and inwards to the highest Dimensional Frequency of your own Being and feel your Oneness - the Oneness of all that is.

For each one of us here tonight is now residing in the Highest Dimensional Frequency of our Soul, but we are not above the Earth Planet, we are within the Heart of the Earth Planet in the embrace of Earth Mother, for *Earth Mother is a Soul Dimensional Frequency of Light, she is the 'essence' of each and every one of you, the 'essence of all that is'.*

Feel the Love, feel the Joy vibrating through the whole of the Dimensional Frequency of Light, rippling through every aspect of your Being. Feel your heartbeat meld with the heartbeat of Earth Mother, for within the heartbeat of Earth Mother lies the heartbeat of the Creator.

You have never left the heartbeat of the Creator, you have always existed within that heartbeat and within the heartbeat of Earth Mother, for although as Humans you tend to look outwards, look beyond yourself for inspiration, for affirmation - the reality is, it is all within the Heart of the Creator and you are a part of that Heart.

Greetings Dear Hearts, I am Ar'Ak, Cosmic brother of this one, and I too am a part of the Heart of the Creator, We all exist within the same High Dimensional Frequencies, we simply move to different Dimensions to experience upliftment, to experience expansion, to experience all we need to become fully functioning within the Heart of the Creator.

You have been told many times that life upon your Planet is an illusion, it is what you have created in order to test yourselves, to enable yourselves to grow into higher and higher Frequencies of Light, higher and higher Dimensions of Soul, but all of it, Dear Hearts, is within the Heart of the Creator.

Feel the pure Love that embraces you at this very moment, allow yourself to experience Divine Love with no limitations, no shadows-Pure Love, Pure Joy.

Those of us, Dear Hearts, who have chosen to grow in other areas of the Cosmos are not separate from you, because the Cosmos itself exists within the Heart of the Creator, so *we are all one*, we simply have chosen to experience our growth in different ways, in different places, and from time to time we come together to exchange our experiences, that each of us may help the other upon their journey. So when your Spirit friends and your Cosmic friends come and speak to you, you are also speaking to them, you are contributing your wisdom to their growth as much as they are contributing their wisdom to yours.

So do not perceive yourselves anymore as being lesser than those you call the Ascended Masters, those you call your Cosmic friends, you are all equal in the Heart of the Creator, fragments of Light intensifying as you grow, and as you grow you contribute greater and greater Light to the Heart of the Creator.

We so love sharing time with you in your Circle of Love, for you have created an environment in which Love and Joy flow so freely, vibrate so highly that you draw to your Circle wisdom from every possible part of the Heart of the Creator.

It is time, Dear Hearts, for you to acknowledge and accept the worth of yourself, the Light within your own Heart, the Wisdom within your own Soul, and to be prepared to share that at every opportunity, sometimes in words, sometimes in actions, but mostly in the energy of Love that you radiate forth to all those upon your Planet, and all those within your Planet, and all those beyond your Planet.

Sit for a moment and allow yourself to *BE* the heartbeat of the Creator and experience the ecstasy and the bliss that is the reality of your Being. All else, Dear Hearts, is the illusion that you have created in order to grow, but now it is time for you to begin to feel and experience the ecstasy and the bliss of being *One with the Heartbeat of the Creator*

Imagine every Star, every Planet, every aspect of the Cosmos being drawn into your Being, into your Heart, everything in perfect Harmony.

FEEL THE HEARTBEAT OF ALL THAT IS, AND KNOW THAT THIS IS YOU.

(21st December 2015)

18

·—·

RE-BIRTHED – RE-AWAKENED

(The Circle opens with the Sounds of the Tibetan Bowls, the Drum and the Blessings Chimes.)

Feel yourselves expanding into the Magenta Light at the Heart of Earth Mother, imagine yourself being cradled gently and lovingly in the arms of Earth Mother, for you have been re-birthed within the *Magenta Light* and you are establishing a new, more loving relationship with the Earth Planet itself, re-connecting with the Love and the Peace that has always been at the *essence* of Earth Mother.

You are all coming home to the Heart of Earth Mother. See yourselves and feel yourselves as infants in your mother's embrace, resonating with the energies of Pure Love. The shadows of your past have been left behind on the old Earth and *you are now re-birthed in Love and Peace.*

Greetings, Dear Hearts, I am Ar'Ak, Spirit brother of this one, this one whom we know as Ra'Zu.

I have to admit, Dear Hearts, we believed for some time that Ra'Zu had chosen to come home, but he seems to have become enamoured with the Magenta Light of the new Earth, so he too has been re-birthed into the arms of Earth Mother.

You are all setting out on a brand new journey, a journey of Love and Peace, a journey of Pure energies, unsullied by the past of Humanity, *re-birthed, re-awakened to the true meaning of Love and Peace and Family,* for yes. Dear Hearts, you are all part of a new family of Humans, *you will completely change the patterns of behaviour upon the Earth.*

Right now, Dear Hearts, you are reaching out to the outer reaches of your Planetary Systems and gazing with wonder at the dwarf Planet Pluto, and you are in awe of what you are seeing, and you are feeling a much greater Love for the whole of the Cosmos, the excitement of new discoveries - *this comes from being re-birthed at this time.*

Each one of you will now look with a baby's eyes at the Planet that you inhabit, the New Magenta Earth, and you will work with Love to create a totally new environment upon the Earth Planet.

As you know from your past existences, growing up is never easy and despite what you perceive as your ages on the old Earth, *you are new-borns on the new Earth* and you will go through a process of growing again, bringing with you the magic and the miracles that unconditional Love creates.

You have seen it many times in the eyes of a child, and now you are feeling it within your own Heart and it is shining out through your own eyes. *You will grow with unconditional Love in your Hearts, and you will establish a new relationship with the Earth Planet that is holding you in its arms.*

Take your time, Dear Hearts, do not feel it necessary to rush and hurry, take your time, allow the Love and the Peace of the Magenta Earth to fill your bones and your veins as you grow into your new journey.

This will be, Dear Hearts, much more a journey of energy than it will be of matter, you have moved beyond the confines of the physical body - the matter that was necessary for your past journeys. You are stepping now into the Dimension of Pure energy and within the purity of that energy there will be no darkness, there will be *Rainbows of Light, Rainbows of Love, Rainbows of Peace,* and you will absorb each and every colour within those Rainbows and *you will grow into magical Beings of Light,* and this time, Dear Hearts, as you grow in the arms of Earth Mother, *you will not forget who you are, you will not forget what you have been, you will not forget what you are to become,* for this is a new partnership. Earth Mother will be always within your Heart and you will Love and Respect Earth Mother like never before.

Take your time, see beyond what you have seen before, *look not with your eyes, look with your Heart* and as you do so, you will begin to act from your Heart and Pure Love will change everything around you.

Dear Hearts, your Cosmic friends, your Spirit friends will continue to work with you whenever you choose to invite them into your Heart, for that is where they belong too, within your Heart, along with beloved Earth Mother.

Allow yourself to open and *Feel the Power of Love,*

UNCONDITIONAL LOVE.

(20th July 2015)

19
. —— .

YOU ARE PERFECT LIGHT
AND PERFECT LOVE

(The Circle opens with the Sounds of the Tibetan bowls and the Blessings Chimes)

Breathe deeply, drawing into yourself the vibrations of Sound, allowing each note to uplift a different part of your physical body into higher frequencies of Light.

Greetings, Dear Hearts, I am Ar'Ak, Cosmic brother of this one.

Embrace the Sound, embrace the Light, feel yourselves moving deeper into your Soul Dimension, elevating your Consciousness into higher and higher frequencies of Light and Sound, that you may feel uplifted and enlightened, One with the Masters and the Angels and all your Cosmic friends who join you within your Circle to share your Loving energies and gift their Loving energies to you in return.

Breathe deeply once more and allow yourselves to float higher and higher into Dimensional Frequencies of Light, to embrace the essence of yourselves, those other aspects of yourselves that are beyond the physical realm and yet are still so much a part of you.

As you walk your journey upon the Earth Planet, you often ignore those aspects of yourselves that are beyond the physical, and yet they move along your pathway with you as Guides, as Angels, as Helpers, as Masters, and all these are part of you.

Breathe deeply once more and embrace the totality of yourself and feel the immediate surge of Joy rising from deep within your physical body and filling every part of you, for it is in the *acceptance of your wholeness that you find the truth of your Being,* that you begin to embrace the different Dimensional Frequencies of Self and recognise your past, your present and your future as One Now Moment.

You are beyond the cares and concerns of the physical realm, you are floating in a sea of Light and Sound that IS complete Joy.

Breathe deeply once more, Dear Hearts, allow this to be the way you feel, allow it to be the whole of you, every atom, every cell uplifted in Light. Let the shadows fall away, let the weight you carry in your physical Dimension fall away, and simply *BE* the highest frequency of Light possible in all Dimensional Realms.

Feel yourselves surrounded and infused with the Blue Light of Peace. Feel yourselves surrounded and infused with the energies of Divine Love. You may think, Dear Hearts, that this is only possible to achieve in your meditative state, but it is not, it is possible for each and every one of you to be constantly in this realm of highest frequency. It will allow you to walk your path with greater ease, for *it is only your own shadows, your own weight that holds you back in the physical Dimension.*

Allow yourselves to rise above the shadows and the weight and focus completely on the highest frequencies of Light.

Take every opportunity, Dear Hearts, to Sound to your Heart, to lift your own vibrational frequencies with the Sound of your voice, the Sound of the bells and the chimes, allowing each to uplift you, so when you look ahead at the pathway before you, you perceive no barriers, your view is completely clear and uncluttered, and Joyfulness will be your constant state, your constant companion.

You do not need to believe, you need to ACCEPT, that you are perfect Light and perfect Love.

Breathe deeply once more and allow the highest frequency of Light in all those around you to meld with yours and to experience the true meaning of *'Oneness'*, and you will immediately see that this is not 'sameness', it is 'Oneness'.

Breathe in, hold, breathe out.
Breathe in, hold, breathe out.

Feel your Heart begin to sing a song of Love and Light to yourself.

Embrace ALL,
BE ALL.

(20th April 2015)

20

·——·

BECOME PURE ENERGY

(The Circle opens with the Sounds of the Tibetan bowls, the drum and the bell.)

As we sit enveloped in the energy of the 'Circle of Joy' we allow the vibrations of the bowls and the drum to uplift each one of us into our Soul Dimension, feeling the perfection that we truly are, acknowledging the infinite Light that resides within our Hearts and vibrating with every breath we take, allowing our energies to flow out across the Earth, and within the Earth, to embrace all as One, and we feel within our Hearts the upliftment of Joy, accepting that this is now the essence of our BEING, the Joy that radiates from the Love and the Peace within our Beings.

Greetings Dear Hearts, I am Ar'Ak, Cosmic Home Trinity brother of 'this one', and I thank you for welcoming me into your Circle tonight to feel the immense power of Joy that resides within each and every one of you, and begins its journey to empower the whole of the Earth.

The whole essence of Ascension, Dear Ones, is the upliftment of Consciousness, and as the Consciousness of each and every individual rises to their Soul Dimension, the whole of the Earth is changed.

You have been told before to move into your Soul Dimension to enable you to look out across the Earth and perceive in a different way the happenings and the events of your Planet, but not as if they are separate from you, but in the *total recognition that everything is ONE with you.*

It is perhaps difficult for your minds to comprehend that you are a part of everything that is happening upon your Earth, for you are still, much of your time, wallowing in judgement-judgement of others, judgement of yourself, judgement of events through the perceptions of separation, and when you have this perception of separation it is then that you begin to feel that you are unable to affect what is happening upon the Earth.

It is only when you accept your Oneness with 'all that is', that you realise that you can and do affect everything that happens upon your Earth. By letting go of judgements and by embracing all in *Love* and *Peace* and *Joy*, you affect everything upon the Earth, you impact everything upon the Earth with the energy you radiate forth.

In your Soul Dimension you accept this Oneness and you radiate to the Earth, through the Earth, with the Earth the beautiful Trinity of *Love, Peace* and *Joy,* and with those pure energies you begin to create the changes that are necessary to lift your Earth from separation, to lift your Earth into Oneness with 'all that is', with the Cosmos.

There are many Beings of Light surrounding your Planet, each offering the *Love,* the *Peace* and the *Joy* within their Hearts to assist the Earth in this time of great change, and *You* as *'way showers'* and *'Light bearers'* are the connection between those Beings of Light and those who are still resting in the darkness of separation.

It is time, Dear Hearts, for each one of you to spend more time in your Soul Dimension and less time in the world of illusion, in the world of separation, in the world of judgment.

Focus on the *Energies* not on the images you see, for they are but illusions, distortions of Light. Focus your intent, your intentions, focus your Heart, your Mind, your Soul on the **Energies** themselves, on the *Energy of Love*, on the *Energy of Peace,* and on the *Energy of Joy,* and then sit and watch as those energies begin to create the New Earth – a New Earth of Oneness, a New Earth of Light.

It is time to let go of the distortions of Light and embrace the Pure *Energies.* As more and more Light flows into the Earth and awakens the *Pyramids of Pure Energy* held within the embrace of Gaia, feel yourself becoming *Pure Energy, Pure Light.* You are the Love and the Peace and the Joy. These are not energies that are separate from you, *these are you!,* for *You, Dear Hearts, are Pure Energy, Pure Light,* and once you embrace that reality you become One with the energies flowing to the Earth from your Sun and from other parts of your Cosmos.

Work through your Hearts and your Souls and

BECOME PURE ENERGY.

(18th November 2013)

21

.———.

'MOTIVATION'

(The Circle opens with the Sounds of the Tibetan Bowls and the Blessings Chimes)

Greetings my friends, I am Ar'Ak-Cosmic Home Trinity Brother of this one, through whom I speak tonight.

I come to speak to you about 'motivation'. Throughout most of this year, you have been receiving messages designed to assist you in changing your perspectives and your attitudes towards your journey on this Planet.

Attitude and perspective are the beginnings of creating the change that is taking place upon the Earth, but attitude and perspective must move forward into *'motivation'*.

How often, Dear Ones, do you take the time to sit back and ask yourself "why am I doing this? What is my motive in pursuing this particular part of the journey, or that particular part of the journey?"

In most instances, Dear Ones, it is probable that you never ask yourself that question. You simply move through your lives the way that you have always done.

So I am here tonight to ask you to place within your Heart the concept of 'motivation'.

A change in attitude creates a change in motivation in your life's journey.

Some considerable time ago, I placed within the Consciousness of Humanity the following statement –

> *If I work for your approval and receive it,*
>
> *My life is enhanced for a moment, but*
>
> *If I work for your benefit and achieve it,*
>
> *My life is enhanced for eternity.*

I ask you to take that statement now and place it within your Hearts for guidance in terms of motivation. For in that statement I am saying to you "If your motivation in what you do is to please others, or to receive congratulations, or affirmations from others, your pleasure will be fleeting, but if the motivation of your actions are to *serve* another, you will be blessed eternally".

It is time to remember, Dear Ones, that you have chosen to come to the Earth Planet at this time, to be *"in service"* to the Earth. So the motivation of everything you do should be the motivation of being *"in service"* to the Earth and to Humanity.

Through eons of time working within the duality of your Planet, within the hierarchical structures of your Planet, the concept of "being in service" has been placed very low on the rungs of the ladders, because "being in service" is being confused within the minds of Humanity with "being in servitude", with having no power, with being repressed in some way, and yet, Dear Ones, "being in service" is the greatest and most noble motivation of all.

All those who have been on your Planet and have moved off your Planet, but continue *in service* to the

Earth – the Masters, the Dragons, the Unicorns, all those who have remained within the Dimensional Frequencies of the Earth, working diligently towards the Ascension of the Planet have been *"in service"* to the Earth, and you also are *"in service"* to the Earth.

It requires a change of attitude to what "being in service" really means. *"Being in service" places the Earth Planet above all else in our life. It is not enslavement, it is complete freedom.*

You have chosen to be "in service" to this Planet, and it is because you are "in service" to this Planet that you are creating the changes within the Earth. You are creating the Ascension of the Earth into its Cosmic frequencies.

So I ask you again to sit within your Hearts and look at your motivation – day in, day out. When you make a decision on some part of your journey, ask yourself "is this decision for the betterment of the Earth, or is this decision for the applause of the those upon the Earth?. *"Do I want a momentary fix, or do I want eternal joy?"*

The subtle changes in attitude that your Beloved friends have expressed to you over a period of the last few months needs now to be acted upon through your *'motivation'*. No one is going to tell you what you should do, Dear Ones, it is the purpose with which you do these things that are the importance.

Take a moment, draw your mind down into your Heart and examine this carefully. *Are you seeking approval, or are you seeking to benefit Humanity and the Planet?*

The statement of which I speak, of course, is another of the 'pearls of wisdom' that you have been given in the past, that has been brought again for your consideration in your new Enlightened states.

So sit with that statement, embrace it, feel it, and allow it to become a part of your life. It is still for you to make the decision, Dear Ones. You can choose the momentary fix, or you can choose the eternal joy. The choice is always yours.

I bless you and I thank each and every one of you for all you have done for this Earth, *and all you will continue to do.*

I thank you.

(14th May 2012)

22

.——.

RELEASE YOUR CONTROL AND
GIFT IT TO YOUR SOUL

(The Balmaceda Tibetan Bowl is Sounded)

Greetings my Dear Friends, I am Ar'Ak, Cosmic brother of this one, and I come to you tonight to offer my apologies, that your Beloved Masters are unable to be with you, but they are deep in conversation, in discussion, in planning for the future of the Earth after the great shift, for yes indeed the Earth has Ascended into a new vibrational frequency.

Although many have not yet felt themselves within that vibration, for as has been customary for Humanity, you lock yourselves within the limitations of your expectations, and you do not allow yourselves to flow freely with the energies of change. You create perceptions within your mind of what will be, and you hold on to these grimly, and when you do not perceive them as happening, you believe that nothing has happened. But I am here to tell you tonight Dear Ones, *everything has happened.* The shift of Dimensions has taken place- for Beloved Earth and for all in and upon and within the Earth.

So, it is time to let go of your previous perceptions, to disentangle yourselves from your previous concepts of how things will feel, and how things will be, and what you will do.

There is a period of adjustment, and because the energies of the fifth Dimension are subtle in nature, within the density that is still your Human body, you have not allowed the subtle energies to fully permeate.

It is time to do this, Dear Ones, it is time to embrace all that is, with no preconceived ideas of how that should appear, or how that should be. Let go of everything that you perceived the Ascension to be, and just move deep within your Heart and allow the subtle energies of the new vibrational frequency of the Earth to meld with your Inner Being.

Release your control and gift it to your Soul, for your Soul sees the way ahead, and will guide you with ease and grace in the New Dimensional frequency.

Allow your Hearts to become One with your Soul, and allow your minds to be still, to follow instead of leading in the New Dimensional frequency.

We do not dismiss the power of your minds, Dear Ones, we seek only to harness it to the will of your Soul. The Human mind will continue to be greatly creative if you allow it to be, but it needs to be harnessed to the vision of your Soul.

Dear Ones, have you forgotten; you walked the Labyrinth of Inner Vision. The inner vision, Dear Ones, is your Soul Vision, and it is time now to harness your mind and your Heart to your Soul Vision.

Relax, allow, embrace and feel the joy and the bliss grow within you, without needing to dissect the reasons why. Simply follow your Soul, your inner vision, and ask not why has this happened, or what is happening, simply ask *'how can I assist my Soul to follow its journey into greater and greater Light'.*

When you ask this of yourself, you release yourselves from the entrapments of the past. You release yourself from the anchors of the Dimension of duality, and you begin to operate in the Dimension of Oneness, and you will feel uplifted, empowered, enlightened in ways you have never dreamed of before.

You are beginning your soul's journey, and letting go of your mind's journey.

But take a moment to give thanks to your mind for having brought you to this point in time-for having brought you to the doorway into your Soul, and into your Soul's journey, and then invite your mind to participate in creating the magic that lies ahead, for your Soul journey is filled with magic. It is filled with Love, and Love is the greatest magic of all.

The whole of the Universe is watching with bated breath to see the Earth become the Star that it is intended to be, and to see the whole of Humanity begin to work positively with the Soul's journey of the Earth.

The beloved Masters are gathered together now to see how they can assist with their energies, to ensure that the journey of the Earth's Soul moves smoothly with ease and grace into the future, and each and every one of you as individuals can work with them by opening to your own personal Soul journey - by accepting and embracing your own Inner Vision.

The canvas ahead is clean and pure, untainted by the past. *It is now for you to create the Masterpiece of the life that is to come.*

Blessings be upon each and every one of you.

(14th January 2013)

23

·——·

A PART OF THE CYCLE OF LOVE

(The Circle opens with the Sound of the Blessings Chimes, the Tibetan Bowls and the Drum)

Feel the vibration of Sound activating every Light Particle within your Being, enabling you to become a Star within your own Physical Cosmos, pulsating outwards the Light of Magenta Peace and Divine Love from within your Heart, to share those vibrations of Peace and Love with all others upon the Earth Planet and all others throughout the Cosmos. For the Light you shine from within your Heart spreads out into the Cosmos and it connects and melds and joins with all the other Stars in the Cosmos and flows back into your Heart, empowered, increasing your own Light frequencies and you become a part of this beautiful wave of energy from Earth to Cosmos, from Cosmos to Earth, *A Part of the cycle of Love.*

Greetings, Dear Hearts, I am Ar'Ak, Cosmic brother of this one.

It is so good to be back with you once more, and to feel the powerful energies of change that are radiating forth from deep within the Earth Planet, and from deep within each and every one of you. We know it is difficult for you to see the Light that you are emitting, but we can see and feel these Light Vibrations, these Love Energies, as they build and build within the whole of the Earth and within all of Humanity.

You are constantly being reminded that you are in a time of great change upon the Earth Planet, and sometimes it is easy for you not to be able to see this. Your world continues to focus upon the shadow side of itself, for that is where you have been living and where you have been looking for so long, for you have not yet completely changed your perspectives and your perceptions to look for and find the Light and the Love in everything around you, but this will happen, Dear Hearts.

You are moving quickly into new Light Frequencies, Earth Mother has opened her Heart with the *Magenta Light*, and now the Hearts of Humanity are also being opened and awakened with their own *Magenta Light*, and you are connecting to each other on different frequencies of Light and Sound. This will uplift you in time, but time is not days or hours or minutes, time is simply the *Now, and the Now is eternal*, so do not judge what is happening upon the Earth in terms of your calendars or your diaries, judge what is happening upon the Earth through your Heart, through the energies of Love and Light that you are beginning to sense from all around you.

As you feel uplifted by the energies flowing into the Earth at this time, you too are uplifting the rest of the Earth, and the Cosmos beyond the Earth.

You are receiving interesting glimpses of what the Cosmos offers, what other Planetary systems offer, Your astronomers, your scientists, are discovering more and more about the Planets in your general vicinity and they speak of the possibilities of life on other Planets, but of course, they perceive life through the very limited aspect of Humanity, not even of the other Beings of Light upon your Planet.

They are seeking to find images of themselves. It is time, Dear Hearts, to let go of that limited perception, and to simply open yourself to the magnificence of life in ALL its forms, that may be in the Cosmos.

This is not a criticism of Humanity, it is natural that you will perceive life as you see it upon your Earth, and when you look for life elsewhere you are looking for reflections of yourself, but do not constrict yourself and limit yourself, simply open yourself.

Love what you see as you look out into the Cosmos, Love what you see when you look out across your Earth, Love it unconditionally and it will Love you unconditionally.

The times ahead upon your Planet are times of great revelations. If you look at all these things through the Colour of *Love* you will find beauty and magnificence. If you perceive it through the fear of differences to yourselves, you will withdraw and restrict yourself once more to the isolation of your sole Planet - but that energy is the energy of the past, and it is rapidly fading from the Earth,

There is a new Openness, a new Acceptance, a new Reality of Oneness, that is beaming forth from the Earth like a Lighthouse in the Cosmos, your Light is shining forth and drawing to it Light Frequencies that will assist you to grow and grow more in your Light, and in your Love. Your Spiritual friends are eager to work with you at this time to fulfill the dreams within *you* - not to manipulate Humanity, or any other Light Being upon the Earth, that is not their role-they are here with you now with open arms and open Hearts, and they embrace you and I embrace you with Unconditional Love and with a vibrational frequency of immense power, personal, individual and collective power – *The Power of Love. The Power of Oneness, Embrace it, Dear Hearts,*

Lift your eyes to the skies and embrace the Love that is pouring onto the Earth at this time, and

BECOME THE ONENESS OF ALL THAT IS.

(12th October 2015)

24

. —— .

YOU ARE THE HOME YOU
ARE SEEKING TO REACH

(The Circle opened tonight with several minutes of laughter and Tibetan Bowls and bells chiming.)

Allow those Sound vibrations to flow deep into your Being, uplifting the energies of Joy within yourself.

Feel the pulsation of Joy flowing through every fibre of your Being. Feel any anchors to the past that are no longer necessary for your stability to flow away, to release you into the energies of Joy, and the energies of Love.

Greetings Dear Ones, I am Ar'Ak-Spirit Brother to this one through whom I speak tonight.

I come to speak to you about *'Home'* – a subject that is much on the minds of many on your Planet at this time as you move towards what is perceived as the end times, the coming together of a number of cycles ending. *It is not of course the end times, merely the change of times.*

As you feel the energies of these times flowing to you, uplifting you-your thoughts perhaps turn to home. I need to remind you Dear Ones that you are living in the Dimension of illusion – *the illusion of separateness*-and it is within this illusion that you create the concept of home as being some place outside of yourselves.

The reality of course, Dear Ones, is that *you are the home you are seeking to reach*. For you see, home is simply the creation of oneness within yourself.

Each one of you has a signature vibration, a vibration of Light that defines your origin.

In your world of illusion and separateness, you perceive that vibration as some distant Planet or distant Star or even a distant Sun and of course this is partially correct, as all illusions are partially correct.

You see, home is the Oneness of your frequency.

From the time you came to this Planet of denseness, you have been journeying home, moving slowly, but inevitable into higher and higher frequencies of Light, and *you will be home when you achieve the Quotient of Light within yourself that resonates with your original Light Quotient.*

The physical aspects of Planets and Stars are merely visions of these resonances of Light. For those who perhaps may believe they come from the Pleiades, what they are knowing deep within themselves, is that they resonate at the Quotient of Light appropriate for that particular system, *but that system is within you!*

Everything, external to yourself that you perceive, exists within you.

You have moved from your Planet on many occasions to rest, to recuperate, to plan your next journey, or next portion of your journey, for it is but a single journey divided into many sections.

I ask you tonight to think of Home, to feel the vibration of Home deep within yourself, and to focus on raising your energy, raising your Quotient of Light to that level of resonance that is Home.

You do not need to leave this Planet in order to achieve your journey Home, *you merely need to let go of the illusion of separateness.* You need to reach into your Heart and know the level of Light that is required within you to become *'Home'* once more.

This, Dear Ones, is why whenever you think of Home, your Heart leaps, your Heart expands - for in your Heart you know you are already Home. You have simply not yet acknowledged the level of Light within yourself that you seek.

It is all within you, Dear Ones. As you approach the end times, this time of great change, focus totally on the Light and the Love within your own Hearts, and embrace the Home you yearn for.

It is not out there in the Cosmos, Dear Ones, it is in there in the Cosmos of your Heart. Feel it now, embrace it now, and experience the upliftment of becoming ONE within yourself. Experience the upliftment of being Home once more.

I give you my Blessings. I give you my Love, and I thank you for sharing your lives and your visions with me and with others, but most of all, with yourselves.

(5th December 2011)

25

·——·

THE ACCEPTANCE OF DIVERSITY

(The circle opens with the Sounds of the Tibetan bowls and the Blessings Chimes)

Focus your eyes on the Rainbow of Light before you on the table. Draw each individual Light into the very centre of your Being, and allow it to pulse through your body, creating a Rainbow of Light through every cell of your Being. Absorb each colour one by one and allow them to move to that Chakra which requires that colour at this time.

The Rainbow is the essence of Oneness, bringing together the whole spectrum of colour into One Union within your Heart.

Now close your eyes but still see those coloured Lights vibrating before you, within you, around you, Blessing you with each pulsation of Light Frequency.

Greetings, Dear Hearts, I am Ar'Ak, Cosmic brother of this one.

I come to you tonight as a ***Rainbow from the Cosmos***, bringing to each of you the bright colours of the Stars and the Planets of your Universe and of the Cosmos as a whole. You have already absorbed at the time of your Equinox the New ***Sound of the Earth,*** the beautiful Sound Frequencies of Light, and now, Dear Hearts, cascading down upon your Earth Planet is the colour vibrations of the ***Rainbow of the Cosmos.*** There are many colours within this rainbow that you have never seen before, for within the limits of the Earth Planet there are only a few colour vibrational frequencies that are visible to your Human eyes, but it does not matter that you can not see the brilliant colours of the Cosmic Rainbow, you are still influenced by their vibration, and they bring to you now and to the Earth Planet now a new enhanced colour frequency to uplift the Hearts of everyone upon the Earth.

They come to work in Harmony with the New *Song of the Earth*, the new Sound Frequencies, each Sound becomes a colour, each note becomes a colour, and together they create a dance of unbelievable Light across your Planet. You know, Dear Hearts, when the sun pulsates out enormous waves of Light, your Earth's atmosphere changes that into colourful spectrums of Light at your Poles. You have seen them, or seen photographs of them, the Northern Lights and the Southern Lights, colours you do not normally see, and this is the Light from your Sun coming together with the atmosphere of your Earth that is creating these.

So imagine, Dear Hearts, the pulsations of Light from the Cosmos coming together with the atmosphere of the Earth to create a Cosmic Rainbow, a Rainbow of Oneness and yet a Rainbow of Diversity, indeed, Dear Hearts, within the Rainbow is the essence of Diversity, The Unification of this Diversity is much needed upon the Earth at this time. All too often Humanity regards difference as threatening, when in reality difference, diversity, is something to be embraced. It is a gift to you, each new colour whether this be the colour of a Being or the colour of a Rainbow has the potential to create great Joy within you, *If you do but allow it!*

You know, Dear Hearts, that you are going through considerable change upon the Earth Planet, and within yourselves, and part of this change is the acceptance of Diversity. This is of critical importance to Humanity! - *The acceptance of Diversity.* The Rainbow teaches you this in a very visual way, as you see the rainbows with your eyes you look for the differences in colours, but you do not dismiss any particular colour, you accept all.

Can you accept all within Humanity? That is the question you have to ask yourselves. As you look around the Earth at the changing times, can you open your Hearts to *all* upon the Earth? *can you accept the Diversity, and embrace the Joy of differences? and not feel threatened?*

It is so easy, Dear Hearts, on your Planet to create the energy of Fear, but you, the *'wayshowers'*, you know that the future is Love, and Love can only *Be* if you accept the Diversity of all that is. The Oneness of all that is, is also the Diversity of all that is.

So I ask you tonight to focus on the Rainbow of Light before you, and in your Heart allow that to expand to accept the greater Rainbow of Light from the Cosmos, to enhance the Sound Frequencies that have already been gifted, and allow your Heart to Sing the *Song of the Earth*, to Sing the *Song of the Rainbow*, to embrace – with *Love* – the Diversity upon your Earth Planet.

You find it easy to accept the Diversity in nature, the different trees that may be part of your woodlands and your forests, why is it so hard to accept the Diversity within Humanity itself?

It is time, Dear Hearts, to embrace the *Rainbow of Humanity,* to let go the judgements of the past, and to feel the Divine Love and Divine Peace within your Heart, expanding into your minds and allowing you to see the beauty of Diversity within the *Rainbow of Humanity*

(3rd November 2014)

26

CONSCIOUSNESS OF ALL THINGS

(The Circle opens with the sounds of the Tibetan bowls and the Blessings Chimes)

Greetings, I am Spirit, Spirit of Crystals and Gemstones. Yes, Dear Ones, you are normally used to hearing me speak **TO** David, tonight I have asked to be allowed to speak **THROUGH** David.

I wish to speak to you about the word **'Consciousness'**. It has turned up in a number of your messages tonight, and yet it is a word that is not easily understood. I hope I will be able to illuminate you, rather than confuse you even further.

From time to time in many of your messages you have been told that your World is an Illusion. Your minds can not connect with this, for your mind indicates that everything it sees, everything it touches is real, and of course it is. When you have been told that all is an Illusion, what you are actually being told is that everything is 'Consciousness', and Consciousness comes to you in forms that you are used to within your own Dimension.

I speak to you of Crystals, for that is my part of the Consciousness. As Spirit of Crystals and Gemstones, I am not some kind of Goddess who oversees all Crystal activities on this Planet and other Planets, I am simply part of the Consciousness that *IS* the Crystalline Dimension

Some of you have wondered, do all Crystals have a Consciousness? What if you have a Crystal that suddenly breaks into two, do you have one Consciousness or two consciousnesses? For you see, Dear Ones, you are only seeing the manifestation within your Dimension of the overall Crystal Consciousness.

The Earth itself is Consciousness, and within the Earth there are what you might call sub-stratas of Consciousness. Humans are a group Consciousness, animals are a group Consciousness, plants are a group Consciousness, Crystals are a group Consciousness. Now if you look at Humanity, and I say that Humanity is a group Consciousness, you can then subdivide that Consciousness as well, and you will see that there are different elements. There are elements which are 'Individual' namely each of you, You have a Consciousness of your own, but your Consciousness is still part of the overall Consciousness of Humanity. But even before you go to the vast Consciousness of Humanity, you may look at your Consciousness as part of the group Consciousness that is here tonight, for yes, when you come together, and when you bring your Love together, you create or become a Consciousness of Immense Power, a Group Consciousness. Beyond the Group Consciousness, you may have a racial Consciousness, you may be Australian, you may be English, you may be South African. All these are subs, sub-stratas of 'Consciousness' itself.

The same occurs within the Crystalline Dimension, you have a Crystalline Consciousness which is part of the Earth Consciousness, and within the Crystalline Consciousness you have sub divisions. You have given different names to different types of Crystal formations, and each one of those has a Group Consciousness. Within that group Consciousness, you have individual Consciousness. So you can see that each division of that Consciousness takes on an Identity. You have on the table before you examples of this, you have on your table a Consciousness which is separated into two different aspects, each one taking on a Consciousness of its own, but each being part of the other and each being part of the whole Crystal Consciousness, *(This referred to a Madagascan Celestite cluster called 'Big Brother' that some 12 years ago Divided in two after a ceremony, one part became known as "Neptune" and the other as "Aquarius")*

The changes that are taking place on your Planet now, the energies that are flowing into the Earth at this time are pushing you inexorably towards an understanding of what is beyond that which you **SEE**, that is beyond what you **FEEL**, that is beyond what you **TOUCH.**

When you hold a Crystal in your hand, you feel its energy, you feel its substance, so yes it is 'real' within your Dimension, but more and more you are being asked to move beyond the Physical reality, beyond even the energy reality of a Crystal, and to connect to the Consciousness of the Crystals. Connecting through your Consciousness, not through your minds, for your mind reflects only what you see, what you feel, what you touch. Your Consciousness connects and communicates with the Consciousness of Crystals.

There is mentioned in one of your messages tonight about the Crystalline grid. The Grid is a wonderful word, it means different things to different people, of course. People normally see it in terms of Geometric Patterns, and essentially when you are looking from above you are seeing Geometric Patterns, just as you are with your Crop Circles, but beyond those Geometric Patterns there is a Consciousness that is crying out to connect with your Consciousness. *Because it is only through the connection of Consciousness that you begin to understand the inter-connectiveness of ALL THINGS.*

When you work with your Marine Meditation, you work with the Consciousness of the Ocean. *(Note: back in 1998 the Neptune Crystal mentioned above was taken to the Glastonbury Tor to "Return the Ocean Consciousness to the Sacred Isle of Avalon")* When you recently created your Rainbow Ball of Light to place in the Gulf of Mexico, you placed it in the hands of the *"Consciousness of the ocean"*, not into the ocean itself as a physical reality, but into the Consciousness of the ocean, for it is the Consciousness which directs what happens in that body. It is the Consciousness of Crystals that directs what happens with the crystals themselves. You know that Crystals are receivers and transmitters of energy, and the energies that are flowing into the Earth at this time are both Light and Sound. Crystals embrace both Light and Sound, and radiate forth both Light and Sound.

It is difficult for your minds at times to understand the differences between reality and Illusion. These are just words that you have created, do not forget that! And you have given these words an energy, and you react to the energy of them. If you simply allow your Consciousness to flow, to embrace, to connect, you will gradually receive a greater understanding of *ALL THAT IS*.

Nothing is as it seems, even within your own Dimension.

I ask you simply to look at yourselves or at each other, what you see is the Physical vessel, what you sense is the energy. How often do you look for the

Consciousness? This is part of the transition that you are going through now, Dear Ones, You will begin to connect with people with the Consciousness, not through the body, not through the energy, but through the Consciousness.

I hope I have not confused you too much, but I felt it was important at this time when you are working with the inflow of Light, the inflow of Sound. You are being asked to work with the Crystalline Grid System, with the Sound Grid System, so it is important that you understand what it is you are working with. You are working with the *"Consciousness of the Earth"*. You have given that a name of course, you have called her **Earth Mother**, just as you have called me **Spirit of Crystals and Gemstones**, but we are all simply a part of the "Consciousness", the original Spark of Source.

Consciousness is the direct connection to Source. So when you are next asked to connect with the Crystal Grid System, to put your energies into it, **Do so through your Consciousness.** Go deep into your heart, call out to your own Consciousness, and work through that energy and you will find upliftment of Spirit like you have never experienced before.

I thank you for allowing me to come to speak with you tonight.

My Blessings be with you all.

(5th July 2010)

27

·——·

ALLOW THE EARTH TO SING ITS NEW SONG FOR YOU AND WITH YOU

(The Circle opens with the sounds of the Tibetan bowls and the Tingsha bells.)

We sound each bowl and the Tingsha bell three times to call into the Circle this evening the power of the Trinity, for the Trinity is the base working vibration throughout the Cosmos. It is the beginning of all creations. Feel the vibration of the Trinity of Sound as it calls to every part of you, as it uplifts the very essence of your Being into the higher spiritual frequencies that will begin the Ascension process of the Earth, and all upon and within the Earth.

From the beginning of time the Trinity energy has played a powerful role in manifesting and creating upon the Earth. It has become the symbol of many of your religious beliefs – the Trinity-the Trinity coming into Oneness to create the new.

Greetings Dear Hearts, I am Spirit – Spirit of Crystals and Gemstones. I come to you at this time to thank you for the energies, for the Love, and for the commitment that all of you have shown through eons of time, in bringing this beloved Planet to the point of no return, to the upliftment of the Earth Planet itself into Cosmic Stardom.

You have come together on many occasions, and called into being the energies of Love, the energies of Harmony, the energies of Peace, the energies of Joy, and each of these energies has been accepted into the framework of the Earth Planet, through my children the Crystals.

As you look forward to the time that has been spoken of as the "Great Shift", you will continue, no doubt, to look for the gateways of Cosmic energy flowing into the Earth, but Dear Ones, you have already called that energy into the Earth, and the Earth has already embraced it!.

It is time now to connect your Hearts with the Heart of the Earth, for it is the Earth itself which will create the energy necessary for the Ascension to take place!. The crystalline structure of the Earth Planet has been empowered by the Love that you have called into being, each and every one of you, and as you are well aware, Crystals embrace energy, and Crystals radiate forth energy, amplifying that which it receives, into that which it gives.

So each time you have called Love into the Earth and placed it within the embrace of the Crystalline structure, you have built the Earth Planet to its *'point of no return'*. Yes, the Earth will tremble to some degree, you may not notice it through your dense physical vehicles, but it will change its frequency as it moves into its higher vibration and the Crystals, my beloved children, will be the active part of this process.

Your connection with the Crystalline structure of the Earth is through the Crystalline structure of your own physical vessels, and this too has been imbued with the energies of Love, and your physical vehicle-and the physical vessel that is the Earth-will resonate with the new frequency, the new Sound Vibrations.

Again, Dear Hearts, on many occasions you have come together and called greater Sound Frequencies into the Earth, allowing YOUR physical vessels to absorb the energies coming from the Cosmos, and to transmute these energies into Love and place it within the Earth, for you have all been part of the Oneness, and you will continue to be a part of the Oneness.

This particular Circle has worked with the Ocean Consciousness, and with the Song Lines of the Earth, and as the time approaches of the great shift, I ask you to continue to focus on the Song Lines and the Ocean Consciousness, *the Earth itself.* There will be others who will work with the Cosmic energies flowing into the Earth at this time, for they have different roles to play.

But each one of you here tonight, and many of you listening to this message, or reading this message will know within your Hearts that you are a part of Mother Earth, and your Hearts will connect and resonate with the Sound of the Earth, a Sound which is in the process of changing as the resonance of the Song Lines increases - and the Crystals begin to sing!.

You will feel it within your Hearts, you will hear it within your Souls, and you will become *ONE* with the New Earth Sound Frequencies, and the Oceans of the Earth will carry that sound, and amplify that sound, and the Earth will be stabilized in its new Ascension frequency.

Can you feel the excitement that is mounting within the Earth, mounting within the Crystal structure of the Earth, and mounting within the Oceans of the Earth Planet? *Open your Hearts and allow the Earth to Sing its New Song for you - and with you - as you step forward on the next part of your journeys.*

I thank you all for having embraced my presence for so long. We will continue to play together, to work together and to sing together as we all move as *ONE* into the New Earth Frequencies.

I bless and embrace each one of you.

(26th November 2012)

28

·———·

STILLNESS OF YOUR HEART

(The Circle opens with the sounds of the Tibetan bowls.)

Greetings Dear Hearts, I am Spirit, Spirit of Crystals and Gemstones. I ask each and every one of you to focus your mind on the sound of the bowl, attaching your mind to the vibration of sound, and as the sound begins to fade I ask you to remain attached through your mind to the sound, and allow your mind to move with the sound, becoming quieter and quieter until it becomes a part of the ***Stillness of your Being.***

(The bowl sounds once again.)

Feel your mind becoming quiet, and more quiet, and feel it become One with the Stillness in your Heart, for it is within the Stillness of your Heart that you begin to sense with *ALL* the senses you possess, senses that need no direction, senses that simply exist in multidimensional levels. So as you sit in the Stillness of your Heart you become more and more aware of your multidimensional Being, you become more and more aware of everything around you.

Through eons of time you have resided essentially within your Mental Dimension and perceived yourselves as separate from Mother Earth, and separate from each other, but in the Stillness of your Hearts as you allow your awareness to come to the surface, you begin to acknowledge that you are *One with all that is*, you become aware of your Oneness with those around you, and you feel the empowerment of that Oneness in the Stillness of your Heart.

Now, Dear Ones, I ask you to become aware of a Golden Light moving upwards from the Earth into every aspect of your Being, filling you and surrounding you, and bathing you in beautiful Golden Light, and as you become aware of this Golden Light you feel the Light begin to draw you down into the Earth, into *MY Dimension of Crystals and Gemstones*.

Feel yourselves moving like a cloud of Golden Light down into Mother Earth, moving freely through each level of the Earth, each Dimensional Frequency of the Earth, finding yourselves totally aware of the magical energies of each and every Crystal structure that you touch, for you touch them with the Love in your Hearts, and they touch you with the Love in *their* Hearts, and you feel the empowerment of the Stillness of the centre of your Being, and as you move through the various levels of the Earth, the various *'gardens of crystals'*, greeting each as a Friend, a Guardian, a Guide. You sense the sound of Mother Earth as each crystal speaks to you, vibrates with you.

The deeper you move into the Earth, the greater the Light you find within yourself; the greater the sounds of Joy you hear within yourself, for you are now sensing the power of Unity and Harmony, of Peace and Serenity.

Allow the Golden Light to take you to the Song Lines of the Earth, through the Rivers of Energy that are the arteries of the Earth, and simply allow yourself to BE a part of this Oneness, a part of this Light.

What you assumed in past lives and past existences to be solid, dark, is in fact brilliant Light within the Earth, and you feel the intensity of Love.

You will find many caverns, many tunnels, many walkways, many roads within the Earth and you will meet Beings of Light from many civilizations that have existed on and within the Earth. ALL are part of the One, ALL are a part of YOU, and there is no judgment as you meet and pass on your journey, there is only the embrace of Love, and an acceptance of the Oneness that you share.

(The bowl sounds once again.)

Allow yourself once more to flow with the sound of the bowl as the Gold Light brings you once more to the surface of the Earth to stand once again upon the Earth, but this time with a new awareness, a new understanding of the Oneness you share with your beloved Earth Planet.

Allow your **Heart** to invite your **mind** to embrace the Serenity, the Stillness of the **ONENESS OF ALL THAT IS**.

(5th August 2013)

29

·——·

LISTEN TO THE CRYSTALS
SING TO YOUR HEART

(The Circle opens with the sounds of the Tibetan bowls, the Blessings Chimes and the talking sticks.)

Greetings Dear Hearts, I am Spirit, Spirit of Crystals and Gemstones.

I ask you now to breathe in, hold, breathe out. Breathe in, hold, breathe out.

As you draw the Light into yourself on each breath you take, I ask you to focus your energies on the crystalline structure of the Earth Planet at this time.

Just as you are going through great changes in Consciousness and in your daily lives, so too my children the Crystals are going through changes of Consciousness, moving ever upwards into more and more refined frequencies of Light, for you are **ONE, *you and my beloved children, the Crystals of the Earth, YOU ARE ONE***, and you are growing together, Ascending together, into higher and higher frequencies of Light.

Over eons of time you have perceived yourself as separate from my children, the Crystals, but you are beginning to realise that you are One with each and every one of them, for *you are One with the Earth Planet itself,* and as you feel your own physical vessel vibrate with new frequencies of Light and Love, embrace the Crystals of the Earth, and share and feel the connectedness of this Light and Love. Accept and acknowledge your Oneness with my children, speak to them often, embrace them often, listen to them often.

You are all on a journey, you are all changing and moving and becoming Lighter and Lighter, and taking your place amongst the Stars. Your relationship with my children the Crystals is changing. You are letting go of all thoughts of <u>using</u> Crystals, of perceiving them merely as tools for your use.

As some of you already know, they have always been your friends and companions, not your tools. Feel the new joyful energies radiating forth from the crystalline structure of the Earth speaking to your Heart, connecting to your Soul and feel a new deeper sense of Oneness, a deeper Love.

Many of you in this Circle have worked and played with Crystals for a considerable time, and you have known that your relationship with Crystals is ever changing, as *you* are ever changing.

So tonight I ask you to open your Hearts and embrace fully the whole of the crystalline structure of the Earth, bathe them with your Light, embrace them with your Love, walk with them hand in hand along the pathway of Ascension.

Take a moment now to breathe in, hold, and breathe out, becoming *one* with the Crystals around you, and the whole Crystal grid structure of the Earth Planet. *Listen to the Crystals sing to your Heart, and as YOU sing, allow your resonance to work in harmony with all the Crystals of the Earth.*

Breathe in the energies of the Crystals, feel them loosen any residual darkness within yourself, and breathe out that darkness and watch as the Crystals of the Earth transmute that darkness into Light, transform disharmony into Harmony.

Breathe in, hold, breathe out. Breathe in, hold, breathe out, become a part of ***all that is*** and feel the Love and the Light of my Crystal children surround and embrace you in every moment of every day.

(5ᵗʰ May 2014)

30

.———.

TRANSFORMATION – THE MOVEMENT FROM SEPARATION INTO WHOLENESS

(The Tibetan bowls are sounded three times)

Feel yourselves being drawn through the Sound Waves, into the Light deep within your Hearts, allowing the vibration of those Sounds to awaken every aspect of your Being to the True Light that you are.

Feel your Light begin to dance on the Waves of Sound, vibrating from the depths of your Being out into the Earth, out into the Cosmos, sounding forth the Love and the Light from deep within yourself.

Greetings, I am Spirit-Spirit of Crystals and Gemstones.

I come before you tonight to embrace you with great Joy, and deepest Love in this time of great transition on the Earth Planet.

Your Guides in recent times have sought to give you different perspectives on your existence, allowing you to see your lives in different ways. I too will do the same, for it is important at this time for you to understand that the Crystal Dimension is a Dimension of Unity, of Oneness – a Oneness with many facets.

Within your Earthly Dimension you have sought to identify the facets of the Crystal Oneness as separate entities, for you exist in a world of separation, and we have accepted and acknowledged the divisions that you have placed upon the Crystal Dimension-perceiving each facet of the oneness to be a separate entity, each with a different role, each with a different purpose-but the purpose of Crystal has always been to embrace the Light and to radiate the Light.

The whole of your Planet is comprised of Crystalline Grid Systems, all drawing in to the Earth, the Light of the Cosmos. We are always acting as **ONE**, a Unity of Consciousness - a Unity of Light.

You, as a Humanity Consciousness, are now moving into the Realms of Oneness, setting aside the separateness of the past, and coming into an understanding of the Oneness of all things. We of the Crystal Dimension are delighted to assist you in this, but for the moment you continue to exist in your separateness, and perceive us in that separateness.

You have chosen to work with certain facets of our Crystal Oneness at your upcoming *Marine Meditation*. You will find that the aspects of the Crystal Dimension you have chosen to work with will bring you great Joy and a greater understanding of Transformation.

You have chosen my children the Azurite, the Watermelon Tourmaline, and the Amethyst-still all facets of the ONE for me, but individual entities for you.

Each facet reflects a variety of colours, and *colour and sound resonating through crystals is what is creating the Transformation at this time.*
You have chosen the Blue Light of Peace within beloved Azurite.

You have chosen the pink and the green of Earthly Love and Spiritual Love, in the Watermelon Tourmaline, and

You have chosen beloved Amethyst-greatest of all transformational aspects of the Crystal Dimension – the Violet Flame of Transmutation, and Transformation.

Each of these will move into your Heart and assist you in the Transformation that will occur within the core of your Being, bringing to you an understanding of the Oneness of all things, for *the transformation that you will experience at this time is the movement from separation into wholeness.*

The Transformation is a *Transformation of 'perspective'* yet again, moving you into greater and greater Light, greater and greater understanding of the inter connectedness of all things within the Universe.

We look forward to participating with you,

To working with you,

To holding within you the greatest aspect of Light possible,

To working with the Crystalline aspects of your own Being,

To bring you into the ONENESS OF ALL THAT IS.

As you walk through the Portal of Transformation, the energies of that Transformation will reverberate throughout the Crystalline structure of the Earth.

All will be transformed as ONE.

I thank you for embracing me this evening. My blessings be upon you.

And so it is.

(5[th]September 2011)

31

·——·

LOOK AT THE HIGHEST POTENTIAL OF YOURSELF

(The Circle opens with the sounds of the Tibetan bowls and the Blessings Chimes)

Greetings, I am Spirit – Spirit of Crystals and Gemstones. I come to you tonight through the embrace of my Beloved child, the Selenite, to draw to your attention the need to let go of the fear of failure, for it is the fear of failure that stops you from looking for the highest potential of yourselves.

Over eons of time few have been prepared to look at the tip of the mountain, and by looking at the tip of the mountain to see the highest potential of yourself, for when you have looked upwards at the tip of the mountain, you have often been afraid to move towards that goal for fear of failure.

I am here tonight to let you know that there is no such thing as failure, except as your own judgement of value. The majority of humanity, through eons of time have walked through life looking down at the next step of their journey, ensuring that they do not trip over themselves or over anything else, and because they have been looking down they have failed to see the potential within themselves, for you only find the potential within yourselves when you look up to the highest aspect of your Being.

Looking upwards at the highest aspect of your Being creates a vision of potential in your life.

Beloved Selenite connects you to your Heart Vision – for your Heart Vision has no fear. As it looks upwards to the highest potential of yourself, it does not consider failure; it sees the myriad of potentials within your life, and it allows you to walk forward without fear and look to achieve the highest potential of yourself.

It is time, in this time of change on your Planet, to let go of the fear of failure, to look at the highest potential of yourself and embrace it with love, and move towards it without fear, without expectation of problems.

It is your mind that tells you to look downwards to see where your next step is going to land. It is your Heart which asks you to look upwards, to be empowered by what you see, and to move easily, gracefully towards the highest potential of yourself.

Yes, Dear Ones, upon your Planet there are times that you will trip and fall, but as your Heart lifts again to the highest potential of yourself, you come back to your feet and you move onward again.

If you are mired in the fear of failure, you go nowhere. Upon your Planet, this is a time when "going nowhere" is not an option!!

It is the time to lift your eyes from within your Heart, and see the greatness and the powerfulness of who you really are, and to walk forward in Love, in Peace, in Harmony, in Joy, and most of all in expectation that you will achieve the goal for which you came to this Planet.

You may work with my Beloved Selenite, Dear Ones, and ask that it helps you to erase the fears that cause you to look down at your next step, and instead allows you to lift up in your Heart and see the tip of the mountain beckoning you onwards, giving you a sense of awe, a sense of wonder.

This is the Inner Vision of your Heart. Embrace it, embrace it fully, and let go of the last remnants of the fear of failure. *For in Love there is no failure-you look ever upwards and you embrace the highest aspects of your Being.*

You will find yourself working more and more with many of my children as these changes begin to occur on your Planet, for it is within the structure of the crystals themselves that the new light quotients will begin to impart wisdom.

I embrace each and every one of you from the Light within my Heart and offer you the opportunity to work with my beloved children, and begin with Beloved Selenite that you may lift your head and see what you will become.

And so it is.

(7ᵗʰ May 2012)

32

ENLIGHTENMENT AND ILLUMINATION IS WISDOM ALIGNED WITH UNDERSTANDING WITHIN THE HEART

(The Circle opens with the sounds of the Tibetan bowls and the Blessings Chimes)

Greetings Beloveds, I am Spirit, Spirit of Crystals and Gem Stones. As you have been told previously, when you moved through the Portal of Transformation, you moved from duality into oneness.

As you carried the consciousness of the Crystal Dimension with you, and the consciousness of the Ocean Dimension, these too have moved into oneness, embraced by the consciousness of oneness.

The crystalline grid system of the Earth has fused into Unity, although it will continue to be represented by a variety of facets of the One.

The energies that are coming to the Earth at this time, and in the time between now and the Equinox of next year, are the energies necessary to lead you to Enlightenment and Illumination.

You cannot attain Enlightenment and Illumination until you align wisdom with understanding. The Earth and Humanity is filled with wisdom, but is yet to attain a level of understanding that changes the wisdom into Enlightenment.

The energies that will be coming to the Earth at the 11.11.11, and again at the Solstice, will be the energies that promote a greater degree of understanding.

Understanding is not of the mind,

It is not rational,

It is not reason,

It is not logic.

Understanding is that inner knowing of the Heart. When you are faced with wisdom, and you react automatically with the knowing in your Heart, the wisdom is transformed into Enlightenment and Illumination.

As you come together on these two occasions – the 11.11.11 and the Solstice that follows, I ask you to focus on the understanding within your own Hearts. I ask you to work with the particular facet of the Crystal Dimension that is attuned to your Heart.

You do not need to bury these crystals, you simply need to hold them within your Heart, and allow the understanding that is inherent in the Crystal Dimension to become ONE with your Heart, and to assist you in beginning an understanding of wisdom.

Everything from this time on is about the Heart, about the knowing deep within you-your Inner Vision.

You will continue to receive and absorb energies to assist you in moving along the pathway to Enlightenment and Illumination.

Open your Hearts, bathe your minds with the energies of your Heart, and allow the energies of understanding to flow deep into your Heart, that they might grow, that they may germinate true understanding, true Enlightenment, true Illumination.

The Crystal Grids of the Earth will embrace you on the 11.11.11, and share with you their gifts of understanding.

Enlightenment and Illumination is wisdom aligned with understanding within the Heart.

And so it is.

(7th November 2011)

33

·——·

AMETHYST

(Place an Amethyst Crystal in your left hand to commence this meditation)

(The circle opens with the Sounds of the Tibetan bowl and the Blessings Chimes)

Greetings, I am SPIRIT, SPIRIT of Crystals and Gemstones

I come before you in true Light and Infinite Love to share and guide your exploration of the wondrous beauty of my Earthly Children, the Crystals.

Each Crystal is a unique vibration, and each has its own Guardian to direct its work in the Earth Dimension, but all Crystals are **ONE** with **SPIRIT.**

I ask you now to relax and place your attention on the Crystal you hold in your left hand.

Focus on your breathing, breathe in, hold, breathe out. Breathe in, hold, breathe out. As you breathe in, imagine you are filling your body with a mist of vibrant purple. As you breathe out, imagine all the blockages and imbalances melting from your body. Breathe in the purple mist, breathe out the blockages and imbalances.

Feel a new sense of equilibrium flow through your physical and emotional Being as you become *ONE* with the purple mist. You have now joined the vibration of the Amethyst.

Amethyst is a true child of *SPIRIT*. It is the designated carrier of the purple Ray, and this Ray draws ones attention towards *SPIRIT*. The Crystal that carries this Ray must do everything possible to assist its wearers to focus their attention on *SPIRIT*. For this reason, Amethyst has a strong balancing effect upon and between ones emotions, memory, mind, subconscious, and the physical body. When these are balanced and aligned, a greater flow of *SPIRIT* force can flow into the physical body. *SPIRIT* force is also the life force and the healing force.

The purple Ray, with the Amethyst vibratory rate behind it, opens the circuit of energy flowing through the throat Chakra and out through the brow Chakra. When this occurs people become able to see into their inner worlds. This in turn brings **SPIRITUAL** unfoldment.

Let us experience this together. Take your Amethyst in your left hand and raise it to the area of your throat Chakra, and let it rest there. Ask for the energy of the purple Ray, and the vibration of the Amethyst to flow into your Being. Allow your consciousness to float on that liquid stream of energy deeper and deeper into your Soul Dimension. Feel the calmness that envelops you. Feel the ropes of fear that bind you to past attitudes melt away. Feel the gentle light bathe and heal you. The deeper you move, the brighter becomes the Light, for the purple Ray seeks out and dismantles the shadows that have accumulated over your many lifetimes.

You step from those shadows into a space of infinite beauty, an oasis of Peace and Harmony. There are others within that space, Beings of your Dimension and Beings of other Dimensions, reach out to them, embrace them with your Love. Have you ever imagined such serenity? such a feeling of completeness? Savour it, absorb it, for you will take the essence of it with you when you return to your Earth Dimension. Look around you, perhaps you see your Guide, perhaps you see a long forgotten friend, call out to them in Joy, recognize that they are a part of all that you have become.

This tranquil place is both a retreat and a meeting place. You can choose to enjoy its radiant beauty in solitude, or you can choose to share it with companion Souls from other Dimensions. Either way you will find no discord or disharmony in its embrace, for this is the space of perfect balance within yourself. My child the Amethyst will help you to connect to this space at any time, and draw the benefits of its balanced energies back into your day to day life, for in balance lies healing of infinite power.

For the moment, however, relax and enjoy the solitude or the company, whichever is your choice for tonight.

Once more it is time to begin the return journey to your conscious Earth Dimension, but remember this, the core of your Being is the source and fountainhead of the greatest wisdom that can ever be known. The Amethyst, like all my other Crystal children, do not provide the wisdom for you, they simply provide a vehicle to help you to look inward to the core of your Being and recognize the truth of what you see.

Now, allow yourself to flow gently back along the ribbon of purple, bringing with you some of the tranquillity that you experienced in your inner space. Feel yourself re-connecting with your physical body, and as you do, feel all the elements of disharmony being displaced from your physical Being. Anger, fear, hatred, all melting away.

Focus once more on your breathing. Breathe in, hold, breathe out. Breathe in, hold, breathe out. Now, as you breathe out, allow the new found balance and Harmony to radiate from your Being to embrace the Planet on which you live, for the Earth also needs to be touched by the healing energies of Peace, Love and Harmony.

All are now **ONE** with my child the Amethyst.

I am *SPIRIT.*

SPIRIT of Crystals and Gemstones.

Blessings be upon you.

GLOSSARY

Ascended Masters-Spiritually Enlightened Beings who have previously incarnated in Human form on the Earth but who are now in Higher Dimensional Frequencies.

Harmonics-A race of Universal Beings who assist Planets to hold themselves in balance through their Sound. There were originally 12 Harmonics holding the Earth in Balance, this changed in 2004 to 18 when the new 'Song of the Earth' came into being

Blessings Chimes – A hand held instrument created from wind Chimes which are used to Bless the Earth, the Oceans and all Beings of Light upon the Earth.

Crystalline Grid – A structured network of Crystals throughout the Earth that are part of the electromagnetic composition of the Earth.

Songlines – there are 12 major songlines throughout the Earth which come together at two places, Sundown Hill just outside Broken Hill in Australia (they are represented here by Sculptures) and Machu Picchu in Peru. They are vibrational, or Sound Arteries of the Planet.

Isle of Avalon – A sacred Site at Glastonbury in the United Kingdom. The Glastonbury Tor is the remnant of this Island that housed the Divine Feminine aspects of the 'old Earth' religions. It continues to exist, but in another Dimensional form and is a 'gateway' to other Dimensions. It is also regarded as the **HEART CHAKRA** of the Earth Planet.

Equinox-An **equinox** is commonly regarded as the moment when the plane of Earth's equator passes through the center of the Sun's disk, which occurs twice each year, around 20 March and 23 September. In other words, it is the point in which the center of the visible sun is directly over the equator.

Solstice-A **solstice** is an event occurring when the Sun appears to reach its most northerly or southerly excursion relative to the celestial_equator on the celestial sphere. Two solstices occur annually, on about 21 June and 21 December. The seasons of the year are directly connected to both the solstices and the equinoxes.

Marine Meditation – This was a Global Meditation initiated by Beloved Germain to be held at 8pm on each Equinox, wherever people were in the world. It focused on connecting with the **CONSCIOUSNESS OF THE OCEANS**. It ran from March 1991 to September 2012-22 years and 44 meditations in all. See http://www.dolphinempowerment.com/MarineMeditation.htm

New Song for the Earth-(Front cover picture) see next page explanation,

Planet Song – the words on the back cover are from the 'Planet Song' by David J Adams. This song can be heard, and downloaded free of charge at https://soundcloud.com/david-j-adams/planet-song

"NEW SONG FOR THE EARTH" EXPLANATION

As the Earth has been undergoing Dimensional change on an unprecedented scale in recent times, there is a need for a new '**SONG**' for the Earth. It will be created at a special gathering at Shambhala. This 'Song' will not only hold the new Earth in Balance, but will further activate all the 'Songlines' of the Earth that the Indigenous Peoples of the Earth so frequently speak of, and honour.

Although the ceremony is taking place in Shambhala it is also taking place all over the Cosmos, as Shambhala will move from Earth during the ceremony to gather the Cosmic 'Rhythm' necessary to underlay the new melody of the 'Song for Earth' that is being created. It will in effect become the 'Mother Ship' for the New Earth vibration.

The ceremony is taking place at 2 levels ... the first level represents the previous/current Vibration and Song of the Earth. *The second level represents what the Earth Vibration and Song is to become –* (Front cover painting). There are both participants and observers at the ceremony. My Spirit brother and Home Trinity member, Ar'Ak, and my Lemurian Trinity companion, N'Tekha, are both observers and are feeding back to me random impressions of what is taking place. I am given to understand that much in the way of the Aboriginal Corroboree, this ceremony will cover many of our Earth days, perhaps even weeks, as time has no relevance.

I will start with what I have been told of the first level. At the Centre is Beloved Earth Mother. She has taken the form of an *OPEN HEART* ... almost Chalice like in it's appearance .... And into that Heart structure she is absorbing incredible colour and Sound Energies from the Cosmos. Arranged in a circle around Beloved Earth Mother are the 12 original Harmonics that came to this planet at its birth to hold the Earth in Matter and Balance with their Song. They have resided in energy Sound Pyramids at various places on the Planet to this time.

Around the Harmonics are a further two Circles. These are comprised of Earth Walkers. The inner circle is rotating in a clockwise direction and the outer circle in an anti clockwise direction. Each circle comprises 36 Earth Walkers, giving a total of 72 for the Planet.

Arraigned around the outer circle in an 8 pointed star formation are 16 Earth Stewards … we know these Beings as Masters and Arch Angels, but within Shambhala they are referred to as Earth Stewards to denote their commitment to the nurturing and upliftment of the Earth Planet.

This is the complete structure of the first level in its barest form, when one adds the aspects of colour, light, movement and sound that each of the participating Beings brings to the structure, what you get is a pattern or vibrating symbol of extraordinary majesty.

The second level varies from the first level mainly as a result of 'Expansion'. 'Compression' creates density, 'Expansion' creates enlightenment. The Planet has expanded and is ascending into a greater Enlightenment, and the new pattern reflects this fact. It is not yet in position, and anchored, as the new song is not yet complete, however, those present at the ceremony have been given a brief glimpse of what it will be … bit like a trailer for a film!

This is what I have so far. Earth Mother will remain in the form of the *'open Chalice Heart'* drawing ever more Light and Love into the Planet from the Cosmos and from the breath of the Creator. The number of Harmonics to hold the Planet in matter and balance will increase to 18, and instead of a circle they will take the form of a 9 pointed star surrounding the Earth Mother. The two circles of Earth Walkers will be increased in size and number to 72 in each circle, giving a total of 144 Earth Walkers on the Planet. The 8 pointed star of Earth Stewards will remain, but a further 8 pointed star with an additional 16 Earth Stewards will be created around it. Like the circles of Earth Walkers, these two 8 pointed stars will now rotate. The original star in a clockwise direction and the new star in an anti clockwise direction. The new Earth Stewards will include some Beings who have not manifested on the Earth Planet at any time but have volunteered their assistance and expertise for the next crucial stage of the Earth's ascension process, so do not be surprised if you start channeling unfamiliar Beings bringing through incredible new wisdom.

The Gathering at Shambhala took place over the Christmas period of 2003, and in January of 2004

I received the following message from my Cosmic Home Trinity Brother Ar'Ak.

I received the following message during the evening of Tuesday 6th January 2004 from My Spirit brother Ar'Ak. You will see in paragraph 2, the *'Seeds'* of what would later become the ***Blessings Chimes!***

*"**The Song is Sung!!!** The Earth Planet dances to a New Cosmic Rhythm, and vibrates to a New Melodic Sound. The Sound of Earth Mother's vibrant **OPEN HEART.** The Earth Planet is in Balance and Harmony once more.*

*Imagine a Wind Chime composed of 18 Rainbow Strands caressed gently by the **'Breath of the Creator'**, and you have the New Song in Earth Mother's Heart.*

Rejoice .... Open your Heart ....Let the New Song resonate within it. Sing along with Earth Mother ... Let the Cosmos resonate to the Pulse of your own joy filled Open Heart."

Blessings

David J Adams

SONGLINES – NAMES AND
APPROXIMATE ROUTES

We have given names to the 12 Songlines that embrace the Earth Planet based on the names of the 12 Sculpture on Sundown Hill, just outside Broken Hill in New South Wales, Australia. Below we give the approximate routes that the Songlines take between Sundown Hill and Machu Picchu as they were given to us in meditation.

RAINBOW SERPENT: Sundown Hill – Willow Springs – Mount Gee (Arkaroola) – Kings Canyon (near Uluru) – Mount Kailash (Tibet) – Russia – North Pole – via the North American Spine to Machu Picchu.

MOTHERHOOD: Sundown Hill – India – South Africa – follows the Nile River to North Africa – Machu Picchu.

THE BRIDE: Sundown Hill – Pacific Rim of Fire – Machu Picchu.

MOON GODDESS: Sundown Hill – Across the Nullabor to Perth – Madagascar – Mount Kilimanjaro – Egypt (Hathor Temple) – Via the Mary Line to the United Kingdom – Machu Picchu.

BAJA EL SOL JAGUAR (UNDER THE JAGUAR SUN): Sundown Hill – Grose Valley (New South Wales) – New Zealand – Chile – Via the Spine of South America (Andes) – Machu Picchu.

ANGELS OF SUN AND MOON: Sundown Hill – Willow Springs-Curramulka (Yorke Peninsular of South Australia) – Edithburgh (also Yorke Peninsular of South Australia)-Kangaroo Island – Mount Gambier-Tasmania – South Pole-Machu Picchu.

A PRESENT TO FRED HOLLOWS IN THE AFTERLIFE: Sundown Hill – Arltunga (Central Australia) – Through the Gold Light Crystal to Brazil – along the Amazon to Machu Picchu.

TIWI TOTEMS: Sundown Hill – South Sea Islands – Hawaii – Mount Shasta (USA) – Lake Moraine (Canada) – via Eastern Seaboard of USA to Machu Picchu.

HORSE: Sundown Hill – Philippines – China – Mongolia – Tibet – Europe – France – Machu Picchu.

FACING THE NIGHT AND DAY: Sundown Hill – Queensland (Australia) – New Guinea – Japan – North Russia to Finland – Sweden – Norway – Iceland – Tip of Greenland – Machu Picchu.

HABITAT: Sundown Hill via Inner Earth to Machu Picchu.

THOMASINA (JILARRUWI – THE IBIS): Tension Lynch pin between Sundown Hill and Machu Picchu.

HOW TO MAKE YOUR OWN
BLESSINGS CHIMES

Blessings Chimes have a triangular wooden top. Inserted into the underside of the wooden triangle are a series of Screw Eyes with a series of chimes dangling from them with THREE 'Strikers' of your own design. The chimes are of different sizes, thicknesses or metals to provide a variety of Tones (which we created by taking apart a number of different, inexpensive, wind chimes). The Screw Eyes are set out in 5 rows from which the Chimes are hung, a single chime at the tip of the triangle, then 2 chimes, then 3 chimes, then 5 chimes and finally 7 chimes. This makes 18 chimes in all. One Screw Eye from which a 'Striker' hangs is placed between rows 2 and 3, and then two Screw Eyes from which 'Strikers' hang are placed between rows 4 and 5.

The 'Strikers' used in creating our Original Blessings Chime for the Marine Meditation had as decorations a Sea horse, a Unicorn, and a Dragon. The Triangular wooden top has a small knob on it, to hold as you shake the Blessings Chimes to create the vibration and resonance.

Although the original has a triangular Top and 18 chimes, you can vary this to your own intuition. The latest version that has been created for David has an Octagonal top and only 8 chimes and is called 'Peace and Harmony Chimes' rather than 'Blessings Chimes' to reflect it's more subtle Sound. Use your imagination and Intuition.

Blessings of Love and Peace

David J Adams

Printed in the United States
By Bookmasters